QUiLTER's favorites

A Collection of **21 Timeless Projects** for All Skill Levels

EDITORS' PICK **VOL. 1**

Traditional Pieced & Appliquéd

C&T PUBLISHING

Text and Artwork copyright © 2009 by C&T Publishing, Inc.

Publisher: Amy Marson

Creative Director: Gailen Runge

Acquisitions Editor:
Susanne Woods

Editors: Lynn Koolish,
Cynthia Bix, and Teresa Stroin

Proofreader: Wordfirm Inc.

Cover/Book Designer:
Kristy Zacharias

Production Coordinator:
Kirstie L. Pettersen

Production Editor:
Alice Mace Nakanishi

Illustrator: C&T Publishing, Inc.

Photography by C&T Publishing, Inc., unless otherwise noted

Published by C&T Publishing, Inc., P.O. Box 1456, Lafayette, CA 94549

Library of Congress Cataloging-in-Publication Data

Quilter's favorites--traditional, pieced & appliquéd : a collection of
21 timeless projects for all skill levels.

    p. cm.

ISBN 978-1-57120-795-1 (soft cover)

1. Patchwork--Patterns. 2. Quilting--Patterns. 3. Appliqué. I. C & T
Publishing. II. Title

TT835.Q488 2009

746.46'041--dc22   2009013133

Printed in China

10 9 8 7 6 5 4 3 2

The Editors of C&T Publishing are proud to present our first collection of *Quilter's Favorites.*

For this collection we've gathered 21 mostly traditional quilt projects, many of which combine clever takes on some favorite blocks and appliqué motifs with contemporary fabrics and fresh color and piecing combinations.

From easy fused Log Cabins to more challenging paper-pieced Pineapple variations and everything in between, you're sure to find a quilt to showcase your stash and suit your style.

Success is just stitches away with the inspiration and instructions you can always count on in books from C&T Publishing.

CONTENTS

courthouse blues

Beginner
Finished block size: 9½″ × 9½″

Courthouse Blues, 50½″ × 50½″, made by Jan Bode Smiley

This classic Courthouse Steps layout of the Log Cabin block is fun to sew together, and sure to please. Done in incredibly rich green and blue batiks, it's regal enough for any décor.

Materials

Medium-light batik: 2 yards for blocks and sashing

Dark batik: 2½ yards for blocks and binding

Light: a fat quarter (18″ × 22″) for the centers of the blocks

Backing: 3¼ yards

Batting: 58″ × 58″

Other supplies: Threads for piecing and quilting

Cutting

Medium-light batik

Cut 25 strips 1½″ wide.

From the 25 strips, cut 50 of each length:
1½″ × 2″, 1½″ × 4″, 1½″ × 6″, and 1½″ × 8″

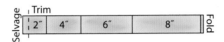

Cutting the medium-light batik

Cut 5 strips 2″ wide, then from these cut 4 strips 2″ × 29″ and 8 strips 2″ × 10″.

Dark batik

Cut 35 strips 1½″ wide.

From 25 of the strips, cut 50 of each length: 1½″ × 4″, 1½″ × 6″, and 1½″ × 10″. From the remaining 10 strips, cut into 50 rectangles 1½″ × 8″.

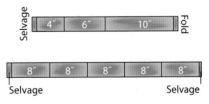

Cutting the dark batik

Cut 4 squares 2″ × 2″ for the sashing corners. Set aside.

Cut 6 strips 2¾″ wide for the binding. Set aside.

Light

Cut 3 strips 2″ wide, then cut the strips into 25 squares 2″ × 2″ for the block centers.

Making the Blocks

1. Use a scant ¼″ seam allowance throughout the block construction. Sew 2 medium-light batik 1½″ × 2″ rectangles to opposite sides of the 2″ center square. Press.

2. Always press the seam allowances toward the most recently added strips.

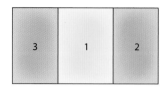

Beginning the block

3. Sew 2 dark batik 4″ strips to opposite sides of the unit. Press.

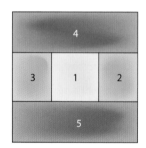

Adding the next strips

4. Sew 2 medium-light batik 4″ strips to opposite sides of the unit. Press.

5. Continue adding strips until the block is complete.

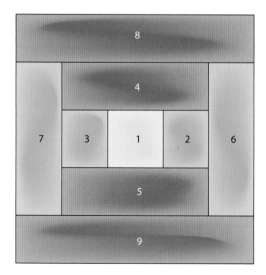

Adding the next set of strips

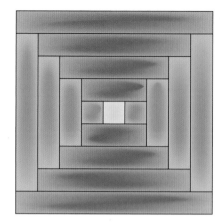

Continue adding strips in the order shown.

Putting the Quilt Top Together

Refer to the Quilt Assembly Diagram (next page) for quilt construction and to General Quilting Instructions (pages 104–109) as needed.

1. Arrange the blocks, sashing strips, and corner blocks on your design wall. Stand back and make sure you are pleased with your layout.

2. Sew the 9 center blocks into 3 rows. Press, alternating the direction of the seam allowances from row to row. This will help make the piecing easier. Sew the center section rows together.

3. For each side of the quilt, sew 3 side blocks together.

4. Sew a 29″ sashing strip onto each set of side blocks.

5. Sew the side blocks and sashing onto the center section.

6. Sew the top row together, then the bottom row. Sew the remaining sashing strips to the corner blocks, then sew the blocks/sashing strips to the top and bottom rows.

7. Sew the top and bottom rows, with sashing, onto the center section.

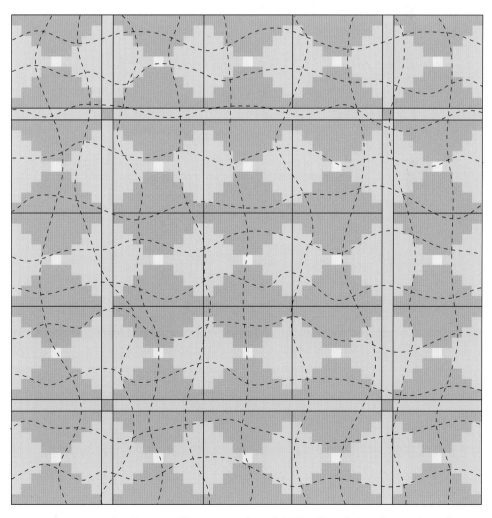

Quilting and Finishing

Refer to pages 105–107 for quilting and finishing instructions.

1. Layer the quilt top, batting, and backing. Pin, thread baste, or use adhesive basting spray.

2. Quilt by hand or machine, using your preferred design, or use the suggested quilting pattern.

3. Trim the excess batting and backing with a rotary cutter, squaring the quilt as you trim.

4. Bind or finish using your favorite method.

Quilt Assembly Diagram

Meandering vertical and horizontal lines create a loose "plaid" quilting design, done with a walking foot and a luscious silk topstitching thread.

winter flowers

Beginner

Finished block size: 9″ × 9″

Finished alternate block size: 4½″ × 9″

Winter Flowers, 64″ × 73″, made by Diana McClun and Laura Nownes, machine quilted by Kathy Sandbach

The large floral border fabric was the springboard for the black-and-white fabrics. Beautiful gold, purple, and red fabrics were added to represent the flowers within the blocks. The fabrics with music and bare branches were selected to enhance the winter theme.

Materials

Based on 42″-wide fabric, from selvage to selvage.

	Photo quilt	Queen	King
Finished size:	64″ × 73″	82″ × 86½″	100″ × 100″
Blocks set	5 × 4	7 × 5	9 × 6
Number of Square-in-a-Square blocks	20	35	54
Number of alternate blocks	20	35	54
Square-in-a-Square blocks:			
Center fabrics (two) **each**	¼	¼	⅜
Light fabric	¾	1⅛	1¾
Dark fabrics (two) **each**	¾	1⅛	1¾
Alternate blocks:			
Five fabrics **each**	⅜	⅜	½
Inner border:			
Cut crosswise	½	⅝	¾
Outer border:			
Cut crosswise	1¾	2	2½
or Cut lengthwise	2⅛	2½	3
Backing	4	7¼	9
Binding (¼″ finished)	½	⅝	¾

Cutting

	Photo quilt	Queen	King
Square-in-a-Square blocks:			
Centers: Number of 3½″ strips from **each** fabric	1	2	3
Light fabric: Number of 1½″ strips	14	24	38
Dark fabrics: Number of 1½″ strips from **each** fabric	14	25	38
Alternate blocks:			
Number of 5″ strips from **each**	2	2	3
Cut strips into 5″ × 9½″ pieces.			
Inner border:			
Number of 2½″ strips	6	7	9
Outer border:			
Cut crosswise: Number of 8″ strips	7	8	11
or Cut lengthwise: Number of 8″ strips	4	4	4

Making the Blocks

Make the required number of Square-in-a-Square blocks for the quilt size you are making.

1. With the right sides together, sew the center squares to a dark strip.

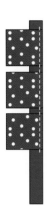

2. Press in the direction indicated by the arrow.

3. Cut the units apart. The new units should measure 3½˝ × 4½˝. Trim to the needed size, if necessary.

4. With the right sides together, place the units onto a dark strip and sew as shown.

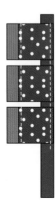

5. Press the seams in the direction indicated by the arrow.

6. Cut the units apart. The new units should measure 3½˝ × 5½˝. Trim to the needed size, if necessary.

7. With the right sides together, place the units onto a dark strip and sew as shown.

8. Press the seam away from the center square as before and cut the units apart.

The new units should measure 4½˝ × 5½˝. Trim to the needed size, if necessary.

9. With the right sides together, place the units onto a dark strip and sew as shown.

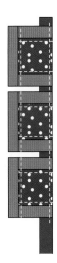

10. Press the strip away from the center and cut the units apart.

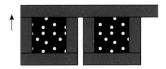

The new units should measure 5½″ × 5½″. Trim to the needed size, if necessary.

5½″
5½″

11. Repeat Steps 1–10, to add the light and then the remaining dark strips. The completed blocks should measure 9½″ × 9½″.

Putting the Quilt Top Together

Refer to the Quilt Assembly Diagram (below) for quilt construction and to General Quilting Instructions (pages 104–109) as needed.

1. A design wall is very helpful when arranging blocks. Refer to the project photo (page 10) for placement of the blocks.

2. Sew the blocks together in vertical rows and then sew the rows together.

3. Attach the top and bottom inner borders and then the side inner borders. Attach the outer borders in the same manner to complete the quilt top.

Quilting and Finishing

Refer to pages 105–107 for quilting and finishing instructions.

1. Layer and baste the quilt. Quilt by hand or machine.

2. Finish the quilt.

Quilt Assembly Diagram

lazy log cabin

Beginner

Finished block size: approximately 6″ × 6″

Lazy Log Cabin, 17″ × 17″, made by Laura Wasilowski

The rich history of traditional quilts is a gift to us all. These sewn, or pieced, quilts are composed of blocks, sets of geometric shapes that form a pattern. The number of beautiful quilt blocks to explore is infinite, and they are often the inspiration for modern quiltmakers. An old standard, the Log Cabin block can easily be adapted to fusing. Making the fused block is similar to the traditional construction process except for one important factor—there are no sewn seams. For the fused Log Cabin, the overlap replaces the stitched seam. Fusing is a fast and enjoyable way to create this time-honored quilt block.

Materials

Center square fabric: 8″ × 8″ of a light value color

Revolving fabrics: 8″ × 8″ each of 6 medium value colors

Background fabric: 18″ × 18″

Backing fabric: 18″ × 18″

Binding fabric: 8″ × 22″

Paper-backed fusible web: 3 yards

Batting: 18″ × 18″

Preparation

Iron fusible web to all the fabrics—except the backing and binding fabric—and remove the paper backing (release paper) in one piece—you will need this to build your Log Cabin blocks.

Making the Blocks

1. Free-cut 1 strip about 1½″ wide, then cut 4 squares measuring about 1½″ × 1½″ from the center square fabric.

2. Free-cut 2 rectangular strips measuring about 1″ × 8″ from each of the 6 revolving fabrics.

3. Free-cut strips measuring about ¾″ × 8″ or ½″ × 8″ from the remainder of each revolving fabric. The Log Cabin design will be more interesting if the revolving fabric strips are not all the same width. To add a little tilt to the cabin, taper the strips from a narrow width at one end to a wider width at the other end.

4. Place a center square fabric in the middle of the release paper (the paper backing from the fusible web). Tack the fabric into place by lightly ironing it to the release paper—this is known as fuse-tacking.

5. Place a revolving fabric strip on the left side of the center square fabric to estimate the length of the center fabric, and cut the revolving strip to that length.

6. Overlap the strip on the center square fabric by about ¼″. Fuse-tack into place.

7. Place a second revolving fabric strip across the top of the 2 joined fabrics to estimate the length of the joined fabrics, and cut the revolving strip to that length.

8. Overlap the second strip on the 2 previously joined fabrics. Fuse-tack into place.

9. Continue to add revolving fabric strips around the collage in a clockwise fashion until the collage measures about 6″ × 6″. The collage does not have to be square.

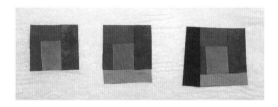

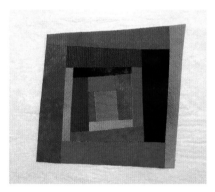

10. After the fabric cools, remove it from the release paper.

11. Make 3 more Log Cabin collages by repeating Steps 4–10.

Putting the Quilt Top Together

1. Center the background fabric on the batting and backing fabric. Fuse-tack into place.

2. Arrange the 4 Log Cabin collages on the background fabric in a grid pattern. Space the Log Cabins about 1½˝ to 2˝ in from the edges of the background fabric.

3. When positioning the Log Cabins, be aware of color placement as well as the relationship that each block has to its neighbor. Shift the Log Cabins until they appear balanced and unified.

4. Fuse-tack the Log Cabins into place on the background fabric.

Quilting and Finishing

Refer to pages 105–107 for quilting and finishing instructions.

1. Press the quilt with steam to set the fusible glue.

2. Layer the backing, batting, and quilt top.

3. Stitch the quilt sandwich together with machine quilting.

4. Trim the quilt square.

5. Add a rod pocket to display the quilt.

6. Bind the quilt.

Variations on a Theme

Traditional quilt blocks provide hundreds of designs that are easily adapted to fused fabrics. Building a traditional block with fusing techniques can be very liberating because there are no templates to follow, seam allowances to adhere to, or measurements to abide by. Experiment with these variations on the Log Cabin block and set yourself free!

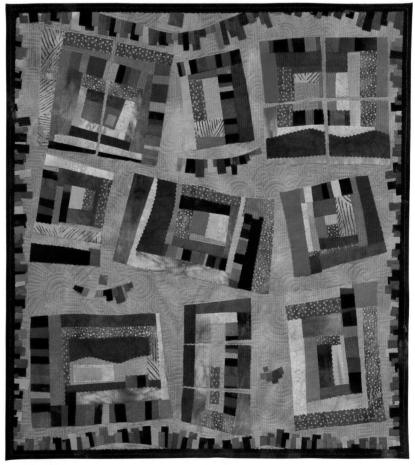

Lazy Log Cabin #3, 23˝ × 25˝, made by Laura Wasilowski

Rail Fence, 16″ × 21″, made by Laura Wasilowski

Select any of hundreds of traditional quilt block patterns and adapt their construction to fusing techniques. Add free-cut elements such as dots or X's to the surface of the block.

Lazy Log Cabin #2, 19″ × 23″, made by Laura Wasilowski

goose in the pond

Goose in the Pond, 57″ × 73½″, made by Becky Goldsmith

This quilt looks more complex than it is. It's basically made up of Nine-Patches and triangle-squares. They combine to make a very interesting quilt.

The scrappy color combination of darker blues with medium to light greens is pretty without being too complex. If you want to introduce more color, make the triangular geese a third color. The Goose in the Pond block is a very traditional design. If you want more color ideas, look at antique quilts to see how other quilters have colored this design.

Materials

This is a scrappy quilt. Use the yardage amounts as a guide. They will vary with the number of fabrics you use.

Greens: A variety of fabrics to total 2⅝ yards

Blues: A variety of fabrics to total 2½ yards

Light block center: ⅓ yard

Sashing: 1 yard

Blue border: ¾ yard

Binding: ⅞ yard

Backing and sleeve: 4½ yards

Batting: 61″ × 78″

Cutting

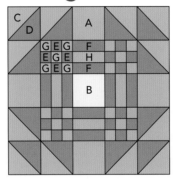

Green fabrics

A, C, and border corners: Cut 18 strips 3½″ × 40″; then cut 196 squares 3½″ × 3½″.

G and H: Cut 15 strips 1½″ × 40″.

Blue fabrics

D and border corners: Cut 14 strips 3½″ × 40″; then cut 148 squares 3½″ × 3½″.

E and F: Cut 18 strips 1½″ × 40″.

Sashing corners: Cut 2 strips 2″ × 40″; then cut 20 squares 2″ × 2″.

Light block center fabric

B: Cut 2 strips 3½″ × 40″; then cut 12 squares 3½″ × 3½″.

Sashing fabric

Cut 16 strips 2″ × 40″; then cut 31 strips 2″ × 15½″.

Blue border fabric

Cut 6 strips 3½″ × 40″.

Binding fabric
Refer to page 107 for making continuous bias binding.

Cut 1 square 27″ × 27″ to make a 2½″-wide continuous bias strip at least 276″ long.

Making the Blocks

1. Set aside 48 green squares 3½″ × 3½″ for A.

2. Make 148 triangle-squares from the remaining green and blue 3½″ × 3½″ squares for C/D in the blocks and the border corners: Place a green square and a blue square right sides together, draw a pencil line from corner to corner, and stitch on the pencil line. Cut ¼″ from one side of the stitched line resulting in 1 triangle-square. Press the seam allowances toward the blue fabric.

note

Be sure to follow these instructions to construct the triangle-squares; this method is different from the method presented in Half-Square Triangles (page 48).

3. Sew a blue 1½˝ × 40˝ strip to each side of a green 1½˝ × 40˝ strip. Make 7 strip units. Press the seam allowances toward the blue fabric.

4. Cut 48 squares 3½˝ × 3½˝ from the sewn strip units for F/H/F in the blocks.

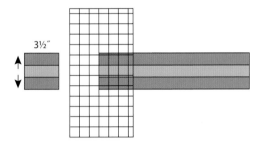

5. Cut 48 strips 1½˝ × 3½˝ from the remaining sewn strip units to be used in the Nine-Patches.

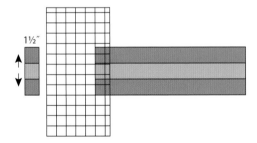

6. Sew a green 1½˝ × 40˝ strip to each side of a blue 1½˝ × 40˝ strip. Make 4 sewn strip units. Press the seam allowances toward the blue fabric.

7. Cut 96 strips 1½˝ × 3½˝ from the sewn strip units to be used in the Nine-Patches.

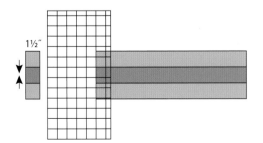

8. Construct 48 Nine-Patches using the 1½˝ × 3½˝ blue and green pieced strips.

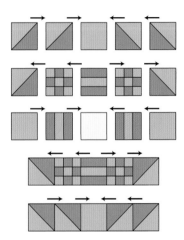

9. Refer to the Goose in the Pond Block Diagram (below), and place the units that make up each block on your design wall. Play with the placement of the units until you are happy with the way the colors are balanced.

10. Sew the units together into rows. The arrows indicate the direction in which to press the seam allowances.

11. Sew the rows together to make the block. Press the seam allowances in the direction indicated by the arrows. Your block should now measure 15½˝ × 15½˝. Make 12 blocks.

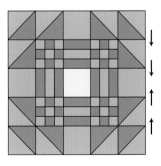

Goose in the Pond Block Diagram

Making the Border

As with all quilts, it is a good idea to measure through the center of your pieced quilt to verify the width and length before you cut the border strips.

1. Cut off the selvages from both ends of the 6 border strips.

2. Sew the strips end to end, right sides together. Press the seam allowances in one direction.

3. Cut 2 strips 3½″ × 51½″ for the top and bottom borders.

4. Cut 2 strips 3½″ × 68″ for the side borders.

Putting the Quilt Top Together

Refer to the Quilt Assembly Diagram (to the right) for quilt construction and to General Quilting Instructions (pages 104–109) as needed.

1. Put all of the blocks, sashing, sashing corners, and border strips and corners on your design wall.

2. Sew the blocks and vertical sashing strips together into rows. Press the seam allowances toward the sashing.

3. Sew the sashing strips and sashing corners together into rows. Press the seam allowances toward the sashing.

4. Sew the Goose in the Pond rows and horizontal sashing rows together. Press the seam allowances toward the sashing.

5. Sew the side borders to the quilt. Press the seam allowances toward the border.

6. Sew the border corners to each end of the top and bottom borders. Be careful to keep the border corners pointed in the correct direction. Press the seam allowances toward the border strips.

7. Sew the top and bottom borders to the quilt, matching the border corner seams to the side border seams. Press the seam allowances toward the border.

Quilting and Finishing

Refer to pages 105–107 for quilting and finishing instructions.

1. Layer and baste the quilt. Quilt by hand or machine.

2. Finish the quilt.

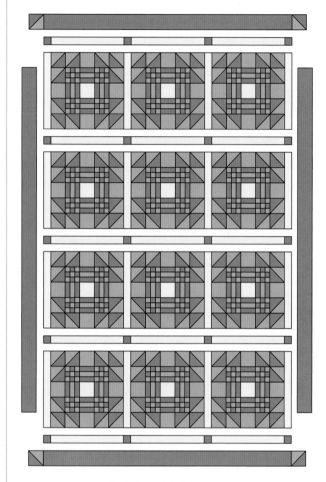

Quilt Assembly Diagram

sunshine and windmills

Advanced Beginner
Finished block size: 6″ × 6″

Sunshine and Windmills, 48½″ × 48½″, made by Karen Dugas, quilted by New Pieces, Berkeley, California

The visual design for this quilt is created when four same-color pieces in the adjoining units touch and form pinwheels. How you see it is not how you sew it. The 6″ pieced unit is constructed from four different color pieces. Each is a part of a different pinwheel.

Materials

Fabric requirements are based on 42″ fabric width.

Pinwheels: ¼ yard each of 21–23 different fabrics **or** 64 scraps at least 4½″ × 16½″

> ### notes
>
> If you have stripes that you want to run lengthwise on the pinwheel, you will need extra fabric; at least 5″ × 16½″ for each pinwheel.
>
> Approximately half of the fabrics are in blue/blue-violet/violet and half in orange/yellow-orange/yellow.

Backing: 53″ × 53″

Binding: ½ yard

Batting: 53″ × 53″

Template plastic

Cutting

PINWHEELS

Use the Pinwheel pattern on the next page.

Cut 4 pieces from each rectangle **or** 12 pieces from each ¼ yard (256 total).

> ### notes
>
> If you stack-cut the pieces, each layer of fabric must be right side up or some of the cut pieces will be backward.
>
> If you use a stripe, fussy-cut one layer at a time to make sure all 4 pinwheel pieces have the same line orientation.

BINDING

Cut 6 strips 2″ × fabric width.
Sew into one long strip.

Making the Quilt Top

Refer to the Quilt Assembly Diagram (to the right) for quilt construction and to General Quilting Instructions (pages 104–109) as needed.

1. Lay out all pieces on a design wall, referring to the project photo (page 23) and the Quilt Assembly Diagram.

2. Stitch A1 to A2 and A3 to A4. Finger-press the seams in opposite directions so the seams will nest.

3. Stitch A1/A2 to A3/A4. Finger press.

Pinwheel unit

4. Repeat to complete 64 units. Press.

5. Sew the units into rows. Press.

6. Sew the rows together. Press.

Quilting and Finishing

Refer to pages 105–107 for quilting and finishing instructions.

1. Layer and baste the quilt. Quilt by hand or machine.

2. Finish the quilt.

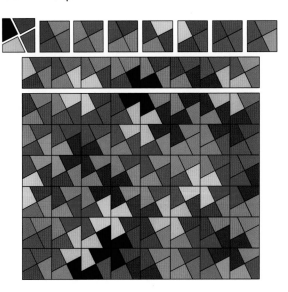

Quilt Assembly Diagram

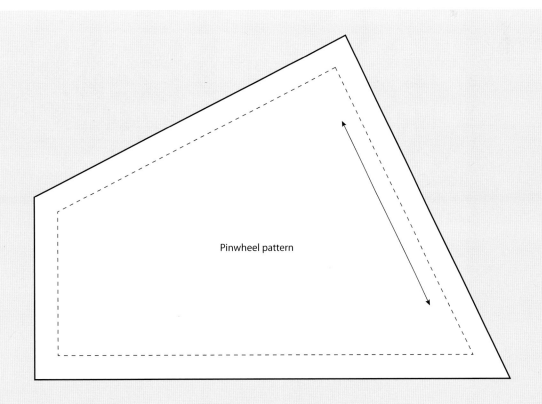

Pinwheel pattern

summer fun

Advanced Beginner
Finished block size: 12˝ × 12˝

Summer Fun, 48½˝ × 61½˝, designed by Jean Wells

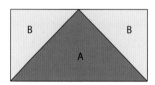

The Double Dutch block generates a lot of movement when you introduce a secondary color pattern, as in *Summer Fun*. The deep blue accentuates the inner pinwheels and heightens the illusion of spinning. A batik fabric in summery blues and greens inspired the palette.

Materials

1⅔ yards green/yellow/blue batik

2⅛ yards yellow batik

1 yard blue batik

1⅛ yards green batik

⅜ yard for binding

3 yards backing

53″ × 66″ batting

Cutting

DOUBLE DUTCH BLOCKS

Green/yellow/blue batik

Cut 8 strips 3½″ × 42″, then cut them into 48 rectangles 31/2″ × 61/2″ (A).

Yellow batik

Cut 8 strips 3½″ × 42″, then cut them into 96 squares 3½″ × 3½″ (B).

Cut 10 strips 2″ × 42″, then cut them into 192 squares 2″ × 2″ (D).

Cut 3 strips 3⅞″ × 42″, then cut them into 24 squares 3⅞″ × 3⅞″; then cut each square diagonally in half (F).

Blue batiks

Cut 8 strips 2″ × 42″, then cut them into 96 rectangles 2″ × 3½″ (C).

Cut 3 strips 3⅞″ × 42″, then cut them into 24 squares 3⅞″ × 3⅞″, then cut each square diagonally in half (E).

Green batiks

Cut 8 strips 2″ × 42″, then cut them into 96 rectangles 2″ × 3½″ (C).

SASHING, INNER BORDER

Green batik

Cut 11 strips 1½″ × 42″, then cut them into 8 strips 1½″ × 12½″ for the vertical sashing and 5 strips 1½″ × 38½″ for the horizontal sashing and the top and bottom inner borders.

Sew the remaining pieces into one long strip. Cut it into 2 strips 1½″ × 53½″ for the side inner borders.

OUTER BORDER

Green/yellow/blue batik

Cut 6 strips 4½″ × 42″. Sew them together into one long strip. Cut them into 2 strips 4½″ × 53½″ for the side outer borders and 2 strips 4½″ × 48½″ for the top and bottom outer borders.

BINDING

Cut 6 strips 1½″ × 42″.

Making the Blocks

1. Stitch 2 B's to each A using the piecing method on page 108 to make 48 large Flying Geese units.

2. In a similar manner, stitch 2 D's to each C to make 96 small Flying Geese units.

3. Stitch the E's and F's together in pairs to make 48 half-square triangle units.

4. Stitch the small Flying Geese units together in contrasting pairs, with the color you've chosen for the inner pinwheel on the bottom.

Make 48.

5. Join the large and small Flying Geese units and the EF half-square triangle units to make 12 Double Dutch blocks.

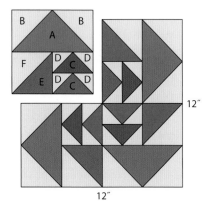

12″

12″

Double Dutch block.
Make 12.

Putting the Quilt Top Together

Refer to the Quilt Assembly Diagram (below) for quilt construction and to General Quilting Instructions (pages 104–109) as needed.

1. Lay out the blocks in 4 rows of 3 blocks each. Stitch the blocks together in rows, inserting vertical sashing strips in between. Press toward the sashing. Join the rows, inserting horizontal sashing strips in between. Press.

2. Sew the top and bottom inner borders to the quilt top. Press toward the borders. Add the side inner borders. Press. Add the side outer borders. Press. Add the top and bottom outer borders. Press.

Quilting and Finishing

Refer to pages 105–107 for quilting and finishing instructions.

1. Layer and baste the quilt. Quilt by hand or machine. The patchwork shapes in *Summer Fun* are outline-quilted, and a sun motif is quilted in the border.

2. Finish the quilt.

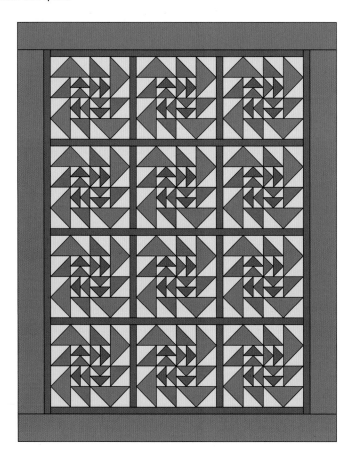

Quilt Assembly Diagram

favorite quilt

Advanced Beginner
Finished block size: 12″ × 12″

Favorite Quilt, 60½″ × 72½″, designed by Jean Wells

Blocks are joined without sashing to create this lively quilt design. The secondary pattern is so strong that it's hard to tell where the original block design begins and ends. The black and cream little prints create the look of an antique quilt.

Materials

Assorted small prints

2⅜ yards total cream-on-black

2¾ yards total black-on-cream

¾ yard total gold

Binding: ½ yard black solid

Backing: 3⅔ yards

Batting: 65″ × 77″

Cutting

Cream-on-black prints

Cut 4 strips 4½″ × 42″.
Cut into 30 squares 4½″ x 4½″ (A).

Cream-on-black *and* black-on-cream prints

Cut 8 strips 4⅞″ × 42″ of each, or 16 total. Cut each strip in half crosswise. Layer the strips right sides together in black/cream pairs, making as many different combinations as possible. Cut into 60 layered 4⅞″ x 4⅞″ squares; cut diagonally in half for 120 layered triangles (B, C). Do not separate the pairs; they are ready for sewing.

Gold *and* cream-on-black prints

Cut 11 strips 1⅞″ × 42″ of each.
Cut each strip in half crosswise (D, E).

Black-on-cream prints

Cut 18 strips 2⅞″ × 42″.
Cut into 240 squares 2⅞″ x 2⅞″; cut diagonally in half (F).

Making the Blocks

1. Stitch the B and C triangles together as paired. Press. Trim the ears.

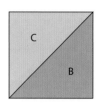

Make 120 assorted.

2. Stitch the D and E strips together in pairs, making as many combinations as possible. Press. Cut each set into 10 segments 1⅞″ wide. Stitch the segments together in random pairs to make 120 Four-Patch units.

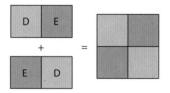

Make 120.

3. Press. Stitch 4 F triangles to each unit. Press.

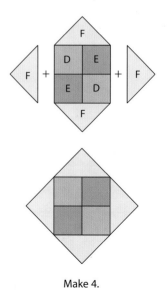

Make 4.

4. Join the A, BC, and DEF units to make 30 blocks. Be sure to position the gold D squares as shown in the project photo (page 29) and block diagram. To ensure a scrappy look and to avoid repetition, lay out and complete four identical blocks at a time. For each new batch of four, choose a different fabric arrangement.

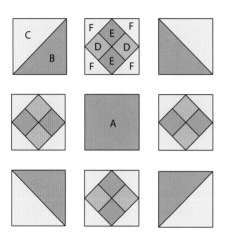

Joining the units

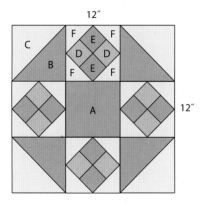

Make 30 assorted blocks.

Putting the Quilt Top Together

Refer to the Quilt Assembly Diagram (below) for quilt construction and to General Quilting Instructions (pages 104–109) as needed.

Place the blocks in 6 rows of 5 blocks each, as shown in the Quilt Assembly Diagram. Stitch the blocks together in rows. Press. Join the rows. Press.

Quilting and Finishing

Refer to pages 105–107 for quilting and finishing instructions.

1. Layer and baste the quilt. Quilt by hand or machine.

2. Finish the quilt.

Quilt Assembly Diagram

jewel box

Jewel Box, 43″ × 43″, interpretation by Donna Ingram Slusser, original design by Carol Honderich

Batik and jewel tone fabrics give the traditional Twelve Triangles block a distinctive, contemporary look. The cool colors of the individual blocks add contrast when placed against the warmer shadow. Carol created this design, which uses only three blocks. It adapts well to foundation piecing. The finished quilt can be turned on point for an alternative and interesting effect. The flat red piping appears as a narrow inner border and accents the overall design.

Materials

Background and inner border*

Light green: 1¼ yards (includes allowance for inner border)

Shadow and flat piping*

Red: 1¼ yards (includes allowance for flat piping)

Purple: ¼ yard

Individual blocks, outer border, and binding*

Dark green: 1½ yards (includes allowance for outer border and binding)

Blue: ½ yard

Backing: 1½ yards

Batting: 47″ × 47″

Fabric amounts allow for cutting border strips and flat piping on the lengthwise grain and for ½″-wide bias binding.

Cutting

All border strips include a few extra inches for length variations. Strips will be cut to the correct lengths before sewing them to the quilt top.

NOTE: The Center Square pattern (page 35) is required for the center square because of its odd size.

Background and inner border (light green)

First cut 4 inner border strips on the lengthwise grain: 2″ × 40″.

Cut 14 squares 2⅞″ × 2⅞″, then cut them in half diagonally.

Cut 14 squares 4⅞″ × 4⅞″, then cut them in half diagonally.

Cut 6 squares 3¼″ × 3¼″, then cut them in half diagonally twice.

Cut 6 squares 5¼″x 5¼″, then cut them in half diagonally twice.

Individual blocks and border (dark green)

First cut 4 border strips on the lengthwise grain: 4½″ × 49″.

Cut 16 squares 5¼″ × 5¼″, then cut them in half diagonally twice.

Individual blocks (blue)

Cut 16 pieces using the Center Square pattern (page 35).

Shadow and flat piping (red)

First cut 4 strips for the flat piping border on the lengthwise grain: 1¼″ × 39″.

Cut 4 squares 2⅞″ × 2⅞″, then cut them in half diagonally.

Cut 4 squares 4⅞″ × 4⅞″, then cut them in half diagonally.

Cut 4 squares 3¼″ × 3¼″, then cut them in half diagonally twice.

Cut 4 squares 5¼″ × 5¼″, then cut them in half diagonally twice.

Shadow (purple)

Cut 2 squares 2⅞″ × 2⅞″, then cut them in half diagonally.

Cut 2 squares 4⅞″ × 4⅞″, then cut them in half diagonally.

Cut 2 squares 3¼″ × 3¼″, then cut them in half diagonally twice.

Cut 2 squares 5¼″ × 5¼″, then cut them in half diagonally twice.

Making the Blocks

BLOCK A: MAKE 4 BLOCKS.

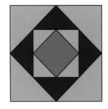

Block A

1. Join 2 light green triangles (cut from 2⅞″ squares) to the blue square as shown. Press. Add 2 more light green triangles (cut from 2⅞″ squares). Press.

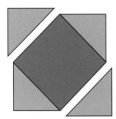

2. Add 4 dark green triangles (cut from 5¼″ squares), using the same technique as shown in Step 1. Press. At this point, all the outside edges will be bias—handle with care.

3. Add 4 light green triangles (cut from 4⅞″ squares) as shown in Step 1. Press.

BLOCK B: MAKE 8 BLOCKS.

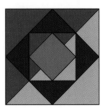

Block B

1. Join the light green and red triangles (cut from 3¼″ squares) as shown. Press.

2. Refer to the Block B illustration for fabric changes, then follow the directions for Block A.

BLOCK C: MAKE 4 BLOCKS.

Block C

Refer to the Block C illustration for fabric changes, then follow the instructions for Block B.

Putting the Quilt Top Together

Refer to General Quilting Instructions (pages 104–109).

1. Arrange the blocks as shown in the project photo (page 32).

2. Sew the blocks together in vertical columns. Press. Sew the columns together. Press.

ADDING BORDERS

Red Flat Piping

1. Measure and cut the final lengths for the four 1¼˝ × 41˝ precut piping border strips (page 104).

2. Press each strip in half lengthwise with the wrong sides together.

3. Align the raw edges of the piping strips with the raw edges of the quilt top, and baste them together using a scant ¼˝ seam allowance.

Light Green Border

1. Measure and cut the final lengths for the four 2˝ × 40˝ precut border strips.

2. Sew the strips to the quilt top using butted corners (page 104). Press.

Dark Green Border

1. The outer border has mitered corners—refer to pages 104–105 before measuring and cutting the final lengths for the four 4½˝ × 49˝ precut dark green border strips.

2. Sew the border strips to the quilt top using mitered corners. Press.

Quilting and Finishing

Refer to pages 105–107 for quilting and finishing instructions.

1. Layer and baste the quilt. Quilt by hand or machine.

2. Finish the quilt.

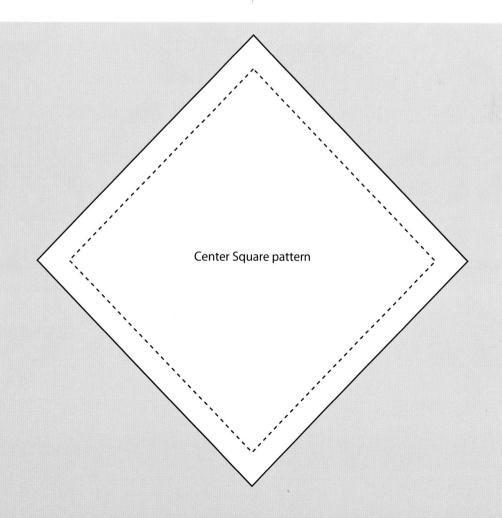

Center Square pattern

making waves

Making Waves, 34½″ × 34½″ , made by Gai Perry

The square size of this quilt makes it a perfect candidate for framing. If your home is decorated with a country theme, the pattern can be turned into the ultimate country quilt by choosing a collection of traditional plaids, checks, stripes, and small-scale prints.

Materials

The use of textured and printed batiks gives the quilt a bold, contemporary look. The complementary color scheme pairs lustrous purples with rich, buttery golds. Notice how the purple color family is stretched to include shades of red-violet and blue-violet. The yellow color family moves from lemon to peach.

Light purple and light gold batiks: ⅛ yard each of approximately 5–6 fabrics of each color family, approximately 1¼ yards total

Darker purple batiks: ⅛ yard each of approximately 10–12 fabrics, approximately 1¼ yards total

Lighter-colored gold batik: ½ yard for block centers and side half-block triangles

Binding: ⅓ yard lighter- or darker-colored batik (No binding is necessary if you are planning to frame this wallhanging.)

Backing: 1⅛ yards

Batting: 38″ × 38″

Cutting

The following cutting method ensures a straight grain is stitched to a bias grain to prevent stretching.

Light purple and light gold batiks: Cut 48 squares 4¼″ × 4¼″ (approximately 24 of each color family), then cut diagonally in both directions. You will need 192 triangles total.

Darker purple batiks: Cut 96 squares 3″ × 3″, then cut diagonally in half. You will need 192 triangles total.

Lighter-colored gold batik: Cut 4 squares 6½″ × 6½″ for full-block centers. Cut 2 squares 9¾″ × 9¾″, then cut each square diagonally in both directions for half-block triangles.

Designing the Blocks

Design four full blocks and eight half blocks. If you are working on a design wall, start by putting up all the pieces for the four full blocks, then add the eight half blocks. Working this way will help you get an even distribution of colors and fabrics. This is important because the quilt will be hanging on the wall for all your friends to see. (Gulp, no pressure here!)

Avoid using the same fabric more than three or four times per block. Use the project photo on the previous page as your reference for placement. Try not to make any two blocks exactly alike.

When all the pieces are arranged on your design wall, squint your eyes (or use a reducing glass) to critique. Rearrange if necessary.

Making the Blocks

1. Sew 4 inner pyramid triangle units. Note that 2 units have 3 dark triangles, and 2 units have 3 light triangles. Press toward the darker triangles. Sew the units to the center square, and press toward the pyramid triangles. Pressing in this direction allows the center square to lie flat and moves the seam allowances out of the way for quilting around the center square.

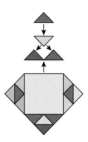

2. Sew 8 outer pyramid triangle units. Note that 4 units have 3 dark triangles, and 4 units have 3 light triangles. Press toward the darker triangles. Sew the units together, and press. Sew the combined units to the block, and press.

3. To make the half blocks, sew 2 inner pyramid triangle units. Note that 1 unit has 3 dark triangles, and 1 unit has 3 light triangles. Press toward the darker triangles. Sew the units to the center triangle, and press toward the pyramid triangles.

4. Sew 4 outer pyramid triangle units. Note that 2 units have 3 dark triangles, and 2 units have 3 light triangles. Press toward the darker triangles. Sew the units to the block, and press.

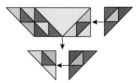

Putting the Quilt Top Together

Refer to the Quilt Assembly Diagram (below) for quilt construction and to General Quilting Instructions (pages 104–109) as needed.

1. Sew diagonal rows of blocks together. Alternate the pressing direction of the seams from row to row.

2. Sew the rows together, and press all the seams in one direction.

Quilt Assembly Diagram

Quilting and Finishing

Refer to pages 105–107 for quilting and finishing instructions.

1. Layer and baste the quilt. Quilt by hand or machine.

2. Finish the quilt.

birds of a feather

Intermediate

Birds of a Feather, 67″ × 73″, made by Becky Goldsmith

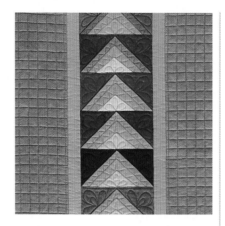

Amish bar quilts are elegant in their simplicity. For this appliquéd version, Becky decided to work within the bounds of that traditional simplicity. She chose to appliqué the Flying Geese, layering triangles of different value and color. There are no center seams in the birds, resulting in a softer appearance.

As you can see, Becky ran out of the primary fabrics she was using for the gold sashing, the green bars, and the blue border. She used the next best fabric that she had on hand. Rather than detracting from the quilt, these new fabrics add a spark of character.

Materials

This is a scrappy quilt. Use the yardage amounts below as a guide. They will vary with the number of fabrics you use. If you run out of one fabric, piece in something similar.

Blue appliqué background: A variety of fabrics to total 2¼ yards

Blue border: 3½ yards

Green vertical bars and largest triangles: A variety of fabrics to total 3 yards

Yellow-green medium triangles: A variety of fabrics to total 1½ yards

Gold sashing and small triangles: A variety of fabrics to total 1 yard

Binding: 1 yard

Backing and sleeve: 5 yards

Batting: 75″ × 81″

Cutting

NOTE: The Flying Geese are appliquéd—add ³⁄₁₆″ turn-under allowance to the patterns for hand appliqué. Use the Bird Block patterns on page 42.

Blue fabrics
Appliqué backgrounds: Cut 68 rectangles 5″ × 8″.
Side borders: Cut 2 strips lengthwise 10½″ × 53½″.
Top and bottom borders: Cut 2 strips lengthwise 10½″ × 67½″.

Green fabrics
Wide vertical bars: Cut 4 strips 5½″ × 40″; construct 3 strips 5½″ × 51½″.
Large Flying Geese: Cut 68 using Pattern 1 (page 42).

Yellow-green fabrics
Cut 68 using Pattern 2 (page 42).

Gold fabrics
Vertical sashing: Cut 11 strips 1½″ × 40″; construct 8 strips 1½″ × 51½″.
Top and bottom sashing: Cut 3 strips 1½″ × 40″; construct 2 strips 1½″ × 47½″.
Small geese: Cut 68 using Pattern 3 (page 42).

Binding
Cut 1 square 29″ × 29″ to make a 2½″-wide continuous bias strip 320″ long. (Refer to page 107 for instructions.)

Making the Blocks

appliqué tip

Use your favorite appliqué technique for the Flying Geese.

keeping track of your blocks

It is always a good idea to audition the background and appliqué fabrics on the design wall before you begin sewing. You may choose to make each bird block exactly the same. In that case it won't matter where any individual block ends up in the quilt. However, if there are differences in the blocks, you will need to keep track of which block goes where.

Number the appliqué blocks from top to bottom by column so you know where to put each block when the time comes. Write the block number in a corner of the background at the edge, where it will be cut off when the block is trimmed.

1. Appliqué the triangles from the top down: stitch #3 to #2, then stitch that combined unit to #1.

2. After the 3 triangles are stitched together, trim the fabric behind each shape, leaving a ³⁄₁₆˝ seam allowance. Appliqué the completed bird to the background.

3. After the appliqué is complete, press the blocks on the wrong side.

4. Trim the blocks to 3½˝ × 6½˝. If you numbered the blocks for sewing, you will cut the numbers off at this point. Write the block number on a slip of paper, and pin it to the block now.

Putting the Quilt Top Together

Refer to the Quilt Assembly Diagram (page 42) for quilt construction and to General Quilting Instructions (pages 104–109) as needed.

1. Arrange all the blocks on your design wall.

2. Sew the bird blocks together into vertical rows. Press in the easiest direction.

3. Sew a vertical sashing strip to each side of the bird bars. Press toward the sashing.

4. Sew the green vertical bars between the bird bars as shown. Press toward the sashing.

5. Sew the top and bottom sashing strips to the quilt. Press toward the sashing.

6. Sew the side borders to the quilt. Press toward the sashing.

7. Sew the top and bottom borders to the quilt. Press toward the sashing.

Quilting and Finishing

Refer to pages 105–107 for quilting and finishing instructions.

1. Use a rotary ruler to draw straight grid lines spaced ¾˝ apart in the green vertical bars.

2. Layer and baste the quilt.

3. Quilt all the seams in the ditch.

4. Quilt the bird blocks with feathers and zigzags.

5. Fill the sashing with 3 lines of channel quilting.

6. Alternate lines of ½˝ channel quilting with 2˝-wide strips of free-motion feathers in the borders.

7. Finish the quilt.

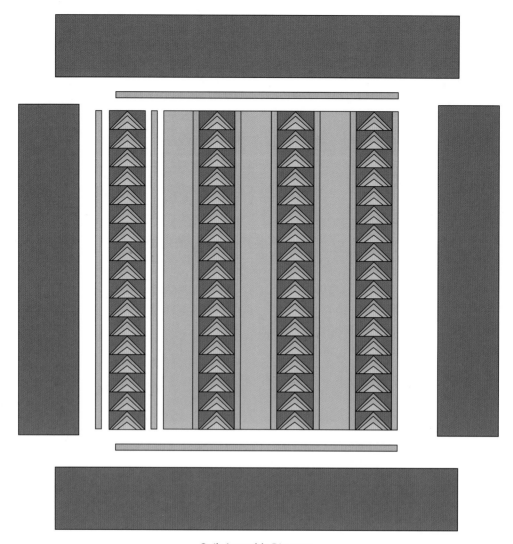

Quilt Assembly Diagram

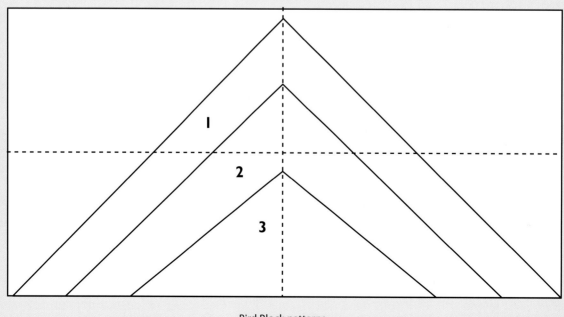

Bird Block patterns

Quilter's Favorites—Traditional Pieced & Appliquéd

castle weather

Castle Weather, 74″ × 74″, designed by Claudia Olson, made by Kathy Storrs

Intermediate

Finished block size: 12″ × 12″

Materials

White (includes binding): 4¼ yards

Light navy: 1⅝ yards

Medium teal: 1 yard

Medium purple: ⅓ yard

Light multicolor: 1¼ yards

Dark navy: 1 yard

Dark teal: ⅝ yard

Backing: 4½ yards

Batting: 78″ × 78″

Cutting

Cut the following 42"-long strips and pieces. Cutting sizes are given in inches.

	Strips		First Cut		Second Cut
Fabric	Number	Size	Number	Size	
Weathervane Block		Finished size: 12″		Make 13.	
White	4	2⅞	52	2⅞ × 2⅞	
	10	2½	156	2½ × 2½	
Light navy	4	2⅞	52	2⅞ × 2⅞	
	4	2½	52	2½ × 2½	
Medium teal	7	4½	52	4½ × 4½	
Medium purple	2	4½	13	4½ × 4½	
Aircastle Block		Finished size: 12″		Make 12.	
White	6	2⅞	72	2⅞ × 2⅞	diagonally once
	2	5¼	12	5¼ × 5¼	
	3	2½	48	2½ × 2½	
Light navy	2	2⅞	24	2⅞ × 2⅞	
	2	4½	12	4½ × 4½	
Light multicolor	3	4⅞	24	4⅞ × 4⅞	diagonally once
Aircastle Block		Finished size: 12″		Make 12.	
Dark navy	2	5¼	12	5¼ × 5¼	
Dark teal	3	4⅞	24	4⅞ × 4⅞	diagonally once
Pieced Border					
White	1	2⅞	4	2⅞ × 2⅞	diagonally once
	8	2½	120	2½ × 2½	
	3	5¼	17	5¼ × 5¼	
	4	4½	60	2½ × 4½	
Light navy	1	3⁵⁄₁₆	4	3⁵⁄₁₆ × 3⁵⁄₁₆	
Light multicolor	4	4⅞	30	4⅞ × 4⅞	diagonally once
	1	5¼	1	5¼ × 5¼	
Dark navy	3	5¼	16	5¼ × 5¼	
	1	3⁵⁄₁₆	4	3⁵⁄₁₆ × 3⁵⁄₁₆	
Outside border and binding					
White (border)	8	1½			
White (binding)	8	2¼			

This quilt is made from two blocks: Weathervane and Aircastle. When the two blocks are placed next to one another, their lines create a zigzag pattern and the shapes appear to fit like puzzle pieces.

Making the Blocks

Press carefully after each step, following the direction of the pressing arrows.

WEATHERVANE BLOCK

1. Position a 2⅞″ white square on a 2⅞″ light navy square, right sides together. Draw a line from corner to corner. Stitch ¼″ on both sides of the line. Cut on the line, and press the units. Make 4 to create 8 half-square triangle units.

2. Sew one unit from Step 1 to a 2½″ light navy square as shown. Make 4.

3. Sew one unit from Step 1 to a 2½″ white square as shown. Make 4.

4. Sew one unit from Step 2 and one unit from Step 3 together as shown. Repeat to make a total of 4.

5. Refer to Quick-Corner Triangles (page 48), and position a 2½″ white square on the upper left corner of a 4½″ medium teal square. Stitch from corner to corner of the white square to make a triangle corner. Trim and press. Repeat to make a triangle on the upper right corner. Make a total of 4 of them.

6. Sew one unit from Step 5 between two units from Step 4. Make 2.

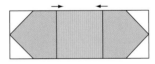

7. Sew 2 units from Step 5 and one 4½″ purple square together as shown.

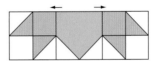

8. Sew the 3 sections together as shown to make the block.

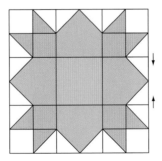

9. Repeat Steps 1–8 to make a total of 13 Weathervane blocks.

AIRCASTLE BLOCK

1. Position a 2⅞″ white square on a 2⅞″ light navy square, right sides together. Draw a line from corner to corner of the white square. Stitch ¼″ on both sides of the line. Cut on the line, and press the units. Make 2 to create 4 half-square triangle units.

2. With right sides together, sew a small white triangle on adjacent sides of the light navy triangle as shown. Make 4.

3. Sew one unit from Step 2 to a light multicolor triangle as shown. Make 4.

4. Refer to Directional Triangles (page 48), and position a 5¼″ white square on a 5¼″ dark navy square. Stitch to the right of the drawn line so the dark navy is on the right. Cut and press.

5. Sew one unit from Step 4 to a dark teal triangle as shown, and press. Repeat to make 4.

6. Refer to Quick-Corner Triangles (page 48), and position two 2½" white squares on opposite corners of a 4½" light navy square. Stitch from corner to corner of the white squares to make triangle corners. Press. Repeat on the remaining corners.

7. Sew 1 unit from Step 5 between 2 units from Step 3. Make 2.

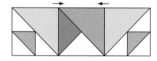

8. Sew the unit from Step 6 between 2 units from Step 5.

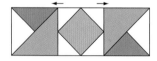

9. Sew the 3 sections together as shown to complete the block.

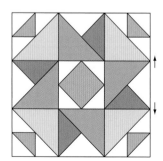

10. Repeat Steps 1–9 to make a total of 12 Aircastle blocks.

Putting the Quilt Top Together

Refer to the Quilt Assembly Diagram (next page) for quilt construction and to General Quilting Instructions (pages 104–109) as needed.

QUILT TOP CENTER

Beginning with a Weathervane block and alternating with the Aircastle blocks, lay out and sew the quilt in five rows with five blocks in each.

PIECED BORDER

1. Refer to Quick-Corner Triangles (page 48), and position a 2½" white square on a 2½" × 4½" light navy rectangle, right sides together. Stitch from corner to corner of the white square. Trim and press the units. Repeat to make a triangle on the opposite corner. Make 60.

2. Refer to Directional Triangles (page 48), and position a 5¼" white square on a 5¼" dark navy square. Stitch to the right of the drawn line so the dark navy is on the right. Cut and press. Make 15 to create 60.

3. Sew one unit from Step 2 to a multicolor triangle as shown and press. Repeat to make 60.

4. Sew a unit from Step 1 to a unit from Step 3 as shown. Repeat to make 60 units, alternating pressing directions.

5. Sew 15 of the units from Step 4 together to create a border strip as shown in the Quilt Assembly Diagram (next page). Repeat to make 4 border strips.

6. As in Step 2, position a 5¼" white square on a 5¼" dark navy square. Stitch to the right of the drawn line so the dark navy is on the right. Cut and press. Make 1 to create 4.

7. As in Step 6, position a white square on a light multicolor square. Stitch to the left of the drawn line so the white will be on the right. Cut and press. Make 1 to create 4.

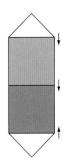

8. Stitch a 3⁵⁄₁₆″ light navy square to a 3⁵⁄₁₆″ dark navy square. Add the small white triangles. Make 4.

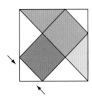

9. Using the units created in Steps 6, 7, and 8, make 4 corner squares as shown.

10. Sew 2 borders to the top and bottom of the quilt.

11. Add a corner square to both ends of the 2 remaining border strips and sew to the sides of the quilt. Press.

OUTER BORDER

Piece the ½″-wide white borders together as needed, and refer to the General Quilting Instructions (pages 104–109) to add them to the quilt.

Quilting and Finishing

Refer to pages 105–107 for quilting and finishing instructions.

1. Layer and baste the quilt. Quilt by hand or machine.

2. Finish the quilt.

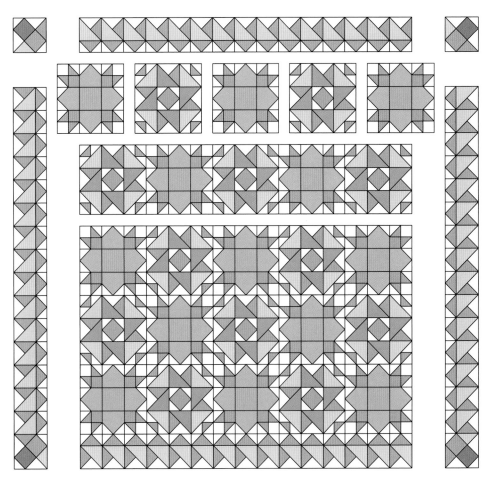

Quilt Assembly Diagram

SPECIAL CONSTRUCTION TECHNIQUES

Half-Square Triangles

1. Layer 2 same-sized squares with right sides together. Draw a diagonal pencil line from corner to corner on the lightest square.

2. Sew a scant 1/4" on each side of the drawn line.

3. Cut on the drawn line, and separate to make 2 triangle units.

4. Press toward the darker fabric unless instructed otherwise.

Directional Triangles

This method is used when the triangles are always in the same position, such as the dark triangle will always be to the left of the light triangle, or visa versa.

1. Layer 2 squares with right sides together, and draw intersecting diagonal lines from corner to corner as shown.

2. Using a scant 1/4" seam, stitch as shown. Rotate the block so that you can use the drawn line as a stitching guide. Follow the project instructions regarding which side of the line to stitch on.

3. Cut along drawn lines, and press open.

Quick-Corner Triangles

Quick corner triangles are made by sewing squares to the corners of larger squares or rectangles.

1. On the wrong side of the square that will become the triangle, draw a diagonal line with a pencil and ruler.

2. With right sides together, position this square on the corner of the piece to which you want to add it. Pin, and sew on the drawn line.

3. Trim the top layer to 1/4" from the seamline as shown. Press the remaining triangle toward the corner.

Trim.

a-tisket, a-tasket, i've got an extra basket!

□□□
Intermediate
Finished block size: 12″ × 12″

A-Tisket, A-Tasket, I've Got an Extra Basket!, 61½″ × 48½″, made by Gai Perry

What a great way to incorporate an extra element in a design! The asymmetry created by the extra basket makes the quilt even more eye-catching.

Materials

This isn't a color scheme for the faint-of-heart so if your comfort level leans toward a more subdued palette, make substitutions.

Blocks

Colorful scraps: Dozens measuring at least 2″ × 2″ in an assortment of light, medium, and dark-bright prints to total approximately 1 yard for baskets

Dark solid: 1¾ yards for basket backgrounds, perimeter triangles, and basket handles

Brightly colored print: 1⅛ yards for block backgrounds

Border

Light, large-scale floral print: 1½ yards

Binding: ½ yard

Backing: 3 yards

Batting: 66″ × 53″

Cutting

Strips are cut crosswise unless otherwise noted.

BLOCKS

Cut the following pieces for each block. You will need 9 blocks.

Colorful scraps
Cut 27 squares 1½″ × 1½″ (A).
NOTE: Use only 2 or 3 of the prints more than once in each block.

Dark solid
Cut 20 squares 1½″ × 1½″ (B).

Cut 1 rectangle 1½″ × 7½″ (C).

Cut 1 rectangle 1½″ × 6½″ (D).

Cut 8 squares 1⅞″ × 1⅞″, then cut in half diagonally to make 16 triangles (E).
NOTE: Two of them will be sewn to the basket handles.

Brightly colored print
Cut 1 square 4⅞″ × 4⅞″, then cut in half diagonally to make 2 triangles (F). (Save the extra for another block.)

Cut 2 rectangles 2½″ × 8½″ (G).

Cut 1 square 6⅞″ × 6⅞″, then cut in half diagonally to make 2 triangles (H). (Save the extra for another block.)

Cut 1 rectangle 1½″ × 9½″ (I).

Cut 1 rectangle 1½″ × 8½″ (J).

Cut 1 square 1⅞″ × 1⅞″, then cut diagonally in half to make 2 triangles (K).

PERIMETER TRIANGLES

Dark solid

Cut 2 squares 18¼″ × 18¼″, then cut in half diagonally in both directions to make 8 side perimeter triangles. (You will not use 3 triangles.)

Cut 2 squares 9⅜″ × 9⅜″, then cut in half diagonally to make 4 corner perimeter triangles.

BORDER

Light, large-scale floral print

Cut 4 strips 5½″ wide.

Cut 2 strips 9½″ wide.

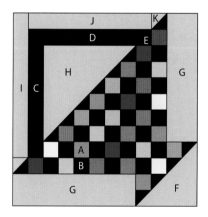

Block Sewing Guide

Designing the Blocks

Arrange all the pieces for the first block on your design wall or board. Now stand back and decide if the assortment of small print squares is strong enough to balance the intensity of the bright background print. If not, make substitutions. When you are satisfied with the first block, sew it using the Block Sewing Guide (above) as a reference. Make 8 more blocks using a different arrangement of colored squares for each block.

Making the Blocks

1. To make Unit 1, sew the 2 E triangles to the C and D basket handles. Press in the direction of the arrows. Sew C/E and D/E to the H triangle. Press. Sew the K triangles to the I and J background rectangles. Press. Sew the I/K and J/K units to the basket handles. Press.

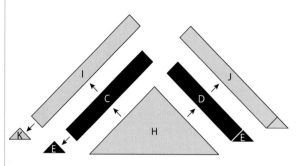

Unit 1

2. To make Unit 2, use the One-Pin, Two-Pin Sewing Method (pages 53–54) to sew diagonal rows of A and B squares and E triangles. Press the seams in opposite directions. Join the rows and press all the seams in one direction. Sew an E triangle to each side of 2 A squares. Press. Sew A/E units to each of the 2 G rectangles. Press. Sew A/E/G units to the basket. Press. Attach triangle F. Press.

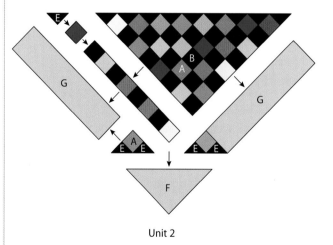

Unit 2

3. Join Units 1 and 2. Press the seams toward Unit 1.

Putting the Quilt Top Together

Refer to the Quilt Assembly Diagram (to the right) for quilt construction and to General Quilting Instructions (pages 104–109) as needed.

1. Arrange the sewn blocks and the perimeter triangles.

2. Start at the lower left-hand corner, and use the One-Pin, Two-Pin Sewing Method (pages 53–54) to sew diagonal rows of baskets and perimeter triangles. Alternate the pressing direction of the seams from row to row.

3. Sew the rows together and press all the seams in one direction. **NOTE:** The bottom of the basket block at the lower end of the second diagonal row will eventually be appliquéd to the border.

4. Piece, if necessary, and trim the border strips to the appropriate lengths. Sew the top and bottom borders and then the side borders to the quilt top. Press the seams toward the border.

5. Turn ¼˝ under on the exposed edges of the lower basket. Using your favorite method, appliqué the edges to the border.

Quilting and Finishing

Refer to pages 105–107 for quilting and finishing instructions.

1. Layer and baste the quilt. Quilt by hand or machine.

2. Finish the quilt.

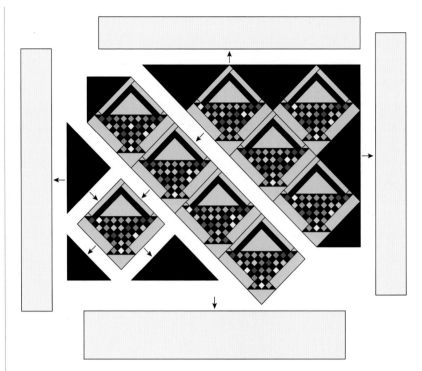

Quilt Assembly Diagram

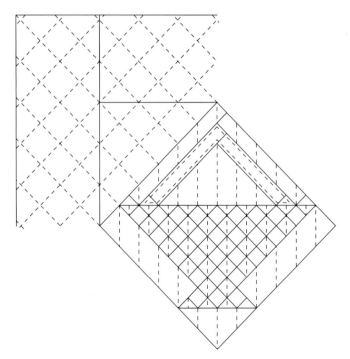

Suggested Quilting Pattern

ONE-PIN, TWO-PIN SEWING METHOD

Here's a method to sew rows of squares together that automatically keeps them in the right order. It's a fast, accurate (and no-brainer) way to sew straight or diagonal rows of squares together. It also works with straight or diagonal rows of blocks. The illustrated directions may look confusing, but if you follow them one step at a time, you will become an enthusiastic convert to the One-Pin, Two-Pin Sewing Method.

1. Begin by putting one pin in the left side of the first square (or block) on the left. This will be called the One-Pin Unit. Now put two pins in the right side of the farthest right square (or block) in the row. This will be called the Two-Pin Unit.

One-Pin Unit   Two-Pin Unit

2. Sew the square (or block) designated as the One-Pin Unit to the square (or block) sitting directly next to it. With the presser foot still down, sew a few more stitches and leave the unit in the machine.

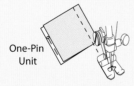

One-Pin Unit

3. From the other end of the same row, pick up the square (or block) designated as Two-Pin Unit and sew it to the square (or block) directly next to it. With the presser foot still down, sew a few more stitches and leave the unit in the machine. With your scissors, detach the One-Pin Unit.

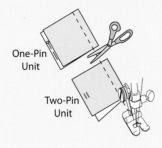

One-Pin Unit

Two-Pin Unit

4. Move back to the left side of the row and pick up the next square (or block) in sequence and sew it to the One-Pin Unit. With the presser foot still down, sew a few more stitches and then leave this unit in the machine. With your scissors, detach the Two-Pin Unit.

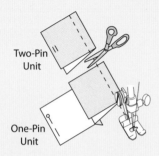

5. Move back to the right side of the row and pick up the next square (or block) in sequence and sew it to the Two-Pin Unit. With the presser foot still down, sew a few more stitches and leave this unit in the machine. With your scissors, detach the One-Pin Unit.

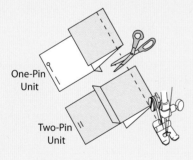

6. Continue sewing in this manner until all the squares (or blocks) in the row are joined to the One-Pin or Two-Pin Units. Sew the two units together and pin the resulting strip on your design wall, or board, in the correct position.

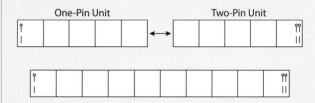

Sewing Diagonal Rows of Squares (or Blocks)

Follow the steps described above. The only difference is that you will put the pins in the triangles at the beginning and end of each row.

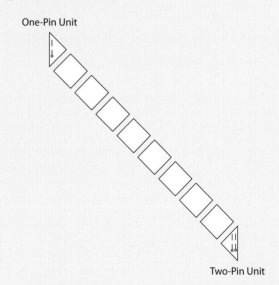

a splash of tulips

Intermediate
Finished block size: 21˝ × 21˝

A Splash of Tulips, 71½˝ × 71½˝, block and quilt designed by Joen Wolfrom, pieced by Polly Keith, machine quilted by Pat Harrison, and bound by Joanne Williams

To make the tulips stand out, it is important to use vibrant colors for the tulip blossoms and the green stems, so there is a definite visual change between the foreground and the background. You can use solid-colored, lightly patterned, hand-dyed, mottled, or other fabrics that give the effect of brightly colored flowers. Use a wide variety of colors for your tulips. The background should be made from a mixture of softly colored fabrics that reflect hints of the flower, leaves, and sky colors. The background fabrics should be neither strongly colored nor strongly patterned. Use as many fabrics as you can. The subtle differences in color, tone, and value in the background fabrics will enhance this quilt's beauty.

Materials

Fabric A: 5¾ yards (total) assorted light yellow, green, aqua, blue, and mauve subtle or tone-on-tone prints for background

Fabric B: ¾ yard (total) assorted medium and dark green prints for tulip bases and stems

Fabrics C: 8 squares 3½″ × 3½″ each of 9 assorted medium and dark purple, pink, fuchsia, red, orange, and yellow prints for tulips (72 total)

Fabric D: 4 pieces 1½″ × 2½″ and 4 pieces 1½″ × 3½″ each of 9 prints in colors to match Fabric C (36 total of each piece)

Fabric E: 4 squares 2½″ × 2½″ each of 9 prints in colors to match Fabrics C and D (36 total)

Border: 1¼ yards leafy green print*

Binding: ⅞ yard

Backing: 4¼ yards

Batting: 75″ × 75″

If you prefer to cut the borders from the lengthwise grain (parallel to the selvage), you will need 2⅛ yards of this fabric.

Cutting

Cut strips on the crosswise grain of the fabric (selvage to selvage).

Fabric A: Cut 134 strips 1½″ × 40″.

Fabric B:
Cut 5 strips 1½″ × 40″.
Cut 36 pieces 1½″ × 3½″.
Cut 36 pieces 1½″ × 4½″.

Border fabric: Cut 8 strips 4½″ × 40″ *

Binding fabric: Cut 8 strips 3¼″ × 40″

If you prefer to cut the border strips from the lengthwise grain, cut 2 strips 4½″ × 63½″ for the side borders and 2 strips 4½″ × 71½″ for the top and bottom borders.

Making the Blocks

To emphasize the tulip shape, use color-matched pieces for Fabrics C, D, and E in each block.

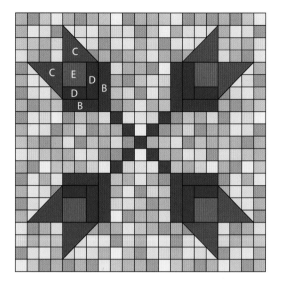

Tulip Block

1. Sew 4 assorted 1½˝ × 40˝ Fabric A strips together to make a strip set; press. Make 31 strip sets. Cut the strip sets into 792 segments, each 1½˝ wide.

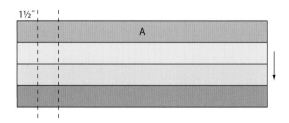

Make 31 strip sets. Cut 792 segments.

2. Sew 3 assorted segments together, mixing and turning them for maximum variety; press. Make 72.

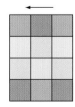

Make 72.

3. Draw a diagonal line on the wrong side of a 3½˝ Fabric C square. Position the square right sides together with the top edge of a unit from Step 1. Sew directly on the drawn line. Trim the excess seam allowance to ¼˝; press. Make 36 of each orientation in color-matched Fabric C sets of 4.

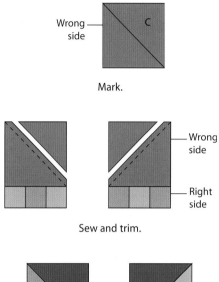

Mark.

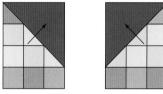

Sew and trim.

Press. Make 36 each.

4. Sew 4 assorted segments from Step 1 together, mixing and turning them for maximum variety; press. Make 36. Repeat to sew 5 segments together. Make 36. Repeat to sew 7 segments together. Make 36.

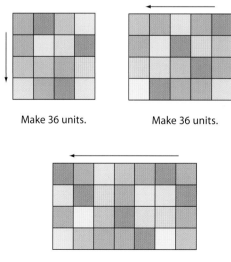

Make 36 units.   Make 36 units.

Make 36 units.

5. Sew 2 Fabric B 1½″ × 40″ strips and 3 assorted Fabric A 1½″ × 40″ strips together to make strip sets as shown below; press. Make 1 of each arrangement. Cut each strip set into 18 segments, each 1½″ wide.

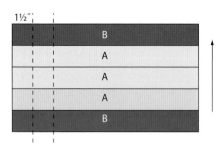

Make 1 strip set. Cut 18 segments.

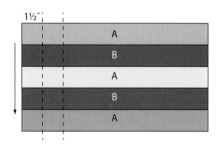

Make 1 strip set. Cut 18 segments.

6. Sew 1 Fabric B 1½″ × 40″ strip and 4 assorted Fabric A 1½″ × 40″ strips together to make a strip set as shown below; press. Cut the strip set into 9 segments, each 1½″ wide.

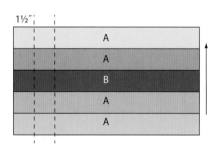

Cut 9 segments.

7. Arrange 2 of each segment from Step 5 and 1 segment from Step 6. Sew the segments together; press. Make 9.

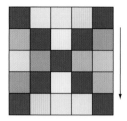

Make 9.

8. Sew a 1½″ × 2½″ Fabric D piece to a color-matched 2½″ Fabric E square; press. Sew a matching 1½″ × 3½″ Fabric D piece to the adjacent side of the unit; press. Make 36 in color-matched sets of 4.

Make 36.

9. Sew a 1½″ × 3½″ Fabric B piece to a unit from Step 8; press. Sew a 1½″ × 4½″ Fabric B piece to the adjacent side of the unit; press. Make 36.

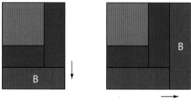

Make 36.

10. Arrange 4 color-matched sets from Steps 3 and 9, 4 of each unit from Step 4, and 1 unit from Step 7. Sew the units into rows; press. Sew the rows together; press open. Make 9 blocks.

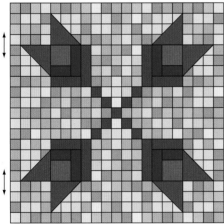

Make 9.

Putting the Quilt Top Together

Refer to the Quilt Assembly Diagram (below) for quilt construction and to General Quilting Instructions (pages 104–109) as needed.

1. Arrange the Tulip blocks in 3 horizontal rows of 3 blocks each.

2. Sew the blocks into rows; press.

3. Sew the rows together; press.

4. Measure, trim, and sew the 4½"-wide border strips to the quilt. Press the seams toward the borders.

Quilting and Finishing

Refer to pages 105–107 for quilting and finishing instructions.

1. Layer and baste the quilt. Quilt by hand or machine.

2. Finish the quilt.

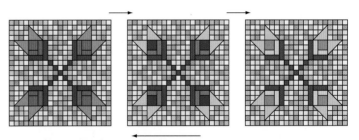

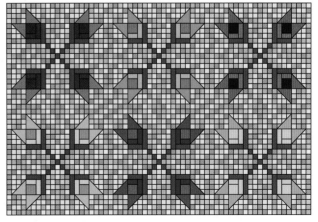

Quilt Assembly Diagram

vinnie's double pinwheel

□□□
Intermediate
Finished block size: 18″ × 18″

Vinnie's Double Pinwheel, 86″ × 109″, made by Nancy Odom, quilted by Linda Leathersich

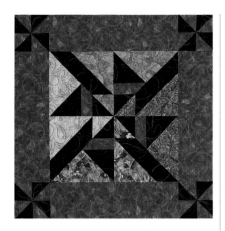

Bold, bright fabrics and sharply contrasting black accents and border give a dynamic emphasis to the large and small pinwheels.

Materials

Blue: ⅞ yard

Orange: ⅞ yard

Yellow: ⅞ yard

Green: ⅞ yard

Red: 3⅜ yards

Black: 5¼ yards (includes binding)

Backing: 7⅝ yards

Batting: 90″ × 113″

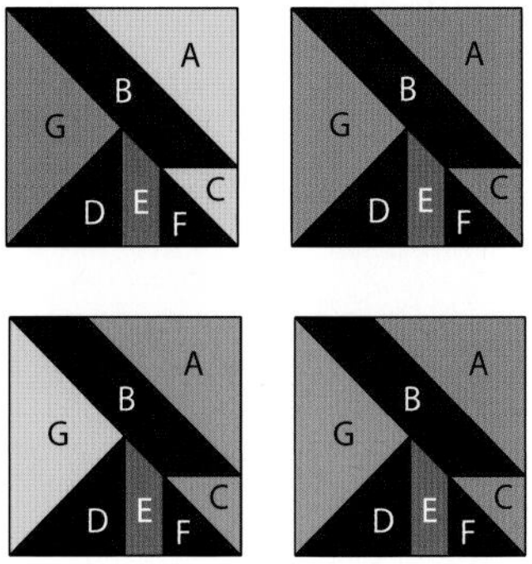

Cutting

Double Pinwheel patterns are on page 64.

Blue

Cut 1 strip 6⅞″ wide, then cut each strip into 6 squares 6⅞″ × 6⅞″. Cut each square in half diagonally to make 12 half-square triangles (A).

Cut 1 strip 3⅞″ wide, then cut each strip into 6 squares 3⅞″ × 3⅞″. Cut each square in half diagonally to make 12 half-square triangles (C).

Cut 1 strip 10¼″ wide, then cut each strip into 3 squares 10¼″ × 10¼″. Cut each square twice diagonally into quarters to make 12 quarter-square triangles (G).

Orange

Cut 1 strip 6⅞″ wide, then cut each strip into 6 squares 6⅞″ × 6⅞″. Cut each square in half diagonally to make 12 half-square triangles (A).

Cut 1 strip 3⅞″ wide, then cut each strip into 6 squares 3⅞″ × 3⅞″. Cut each square in half diagonally to make 12 half-square triangles (C).

Cut 1 strip 10¼″ wide, then cut each strip into 3 squares 10¼″ × 10¼″. Cut each square twice diagonally into quarters to make 12 quarter-square triangles (G).

Yellow

Cut 1 strip 6⅞″ wide, then cut each strip into 6 squares 6⅞″ × 6⅞″. Cut each square in half diagonally to make 12 half-square triangles (A).

Cut 1 strip 3⅞″ wide, then cut each strip into 6 squares 3⅞″ × 3⅞″. Cut each square in half diagonally to make 12 half-square triangles (C).

Cut 1 strip 10¼″ wide, then cut each strip into 3 squares 10¼″ × 10¼″. Cut each square twice diagonally into quarters to make 12 quarter-square triangles (G).

Green

Cut 1 strip 6⅞″ wide, then cut each strip into 6 squares 6⅞″ × 6⅞″. Cut each square in half diagonally to make 12 half-square triangles (A).

Cut 1 strip 3⅞″ wide, then cut each strip into 6 squares 3⅞″ × 3⅞″. Cut each square in half diagonally to make 12 half-square triangles (C).

Cut 1 strip 10¼″ wide, then cut each strip into 3 squares 10¼″ × 10¼″. Cut each square twice diagonally into quarters to make 12 quarter-square triangles (G).

Red

Using the Double Pinwheel pattern E (page 64), cut 48 trapezoids (E).

Cut 4 strips 3⅜″ wide, then cut the strips into 40 squares 3⅜″ × 3⅜″. Cut each square in half diagonally to make 80 triangles for the sashing Pinwheels.

Cut 16 strips 5½″ wide, then cut the strips into 31 rectangles 5½″ × 18½″ for sashing strips.

Black

Using Double Pinwheel pattern B (page 64), cut 48 parallelograms.

Cut 3 strips 3⅞″ wide, then cut the strips into 24 squares 3⅞″ × 3⅞″. Cut each square in half diagonally to make 48 black triangles (F).

Cut 4 strips 5⅜″ wide, then cut the strips into 24 squares 5⅜″ × 5⅜″. Cut the squares in half diagonally to make 48 black triangles for pinwheels (D).

Cut 4 strips 3⅜″ wide, then cut the strips into 40 squares 3⅜″ × 3⅜″. Cut each square in half diagonally to make 80 triangles for the sashing Pinwheels.

Cut 11 strips 6½″ wide for the border.

Making the Blocks

Make 12 of each color: blue, green, yellow, and orange.

PINWHEEL BLOCK ASSEMBLY

1. Sew triangle (A) to black trapezoid (B). Press. Then sew the A/B unit to triangle (C). Press. Make 12 A/B/C units of each color: blue, green, yellow, and orange.

Make 12 of each color.

2. Sew black triangle (D) to red piece (E). Then sew the D/E unit to black triangle (F). Press. Make 48 D/E/F units.

3. Sew a D/E/F unit to a quarter-square triangle (G). Press. Make 12 units of each color: blue, green, yellow, and orange.

Make 12 of each color.

4. Sew the 2 units together to make one quarter of the block. Press. Repeat to make 12 of each color. Refer to the project photo (page 60) for color placement.

Make 12 of each color.

5. Sew the 4 quarters of the block together to complete the block. Press.

Double Pinwheel Block Assembly

PINWHEEL SASHING BLOCKS

1. Sew together black and red triangles to make 40 half-square triangle units. Press the seam toward the black triangle.

Make 80.

2. Sew the units together to make 20 pinwheels. Press.

Make 20.

Putting the Quilt Top Together

Refer to the Quilt Assembly Diagram (at the right) for quilt construction and to General Quilting Instructions (pages 104–109) as needed.

1. Arrange the blocks and sashing.

2. Sew the Double Pinwheel blocks, sashing Pinwheel blocks, and sashing strips into rows. Press the seams toward the sashing.

3. Sew the block rows and sashing rows together. Press the seams toward the sashing rows.

4. Sew the 6½˝-wide border strips end to end, and cut two 6½˝ × 97½˝ side borders and two 6½˝ × 86½˝ top and bottom borders.

5. Sew the borders to the sides and then to the top and bottom of the quilt top. Press the seams toward the border.

Quilting and Finishing

Refer to pages 105–107 for quilting and finishing instructions.

1. Layer and baste the quilt. Quilt by hand or machine.

2. Finish the quilt.

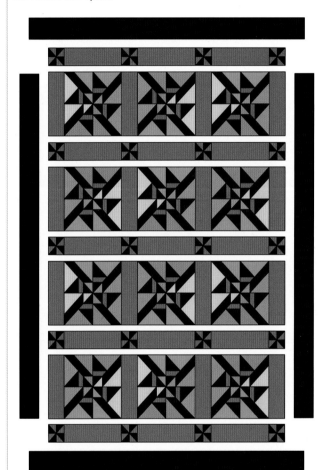

Quilt Assembly Diagram

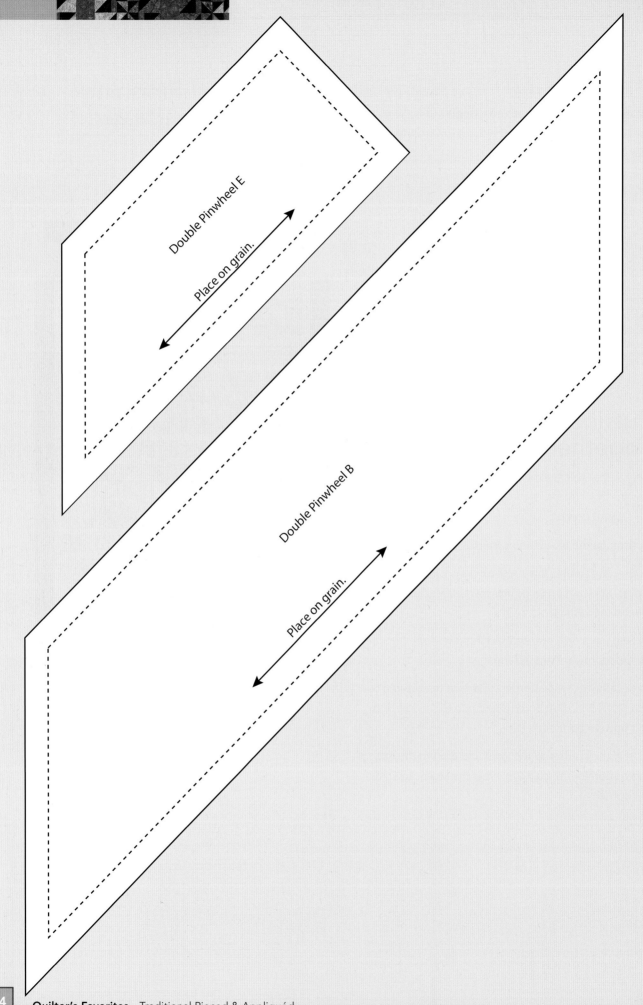

Double Pinwheel E

Place on grain.

Double Pinwheel B

Place on grain.

curvaceous cabins

Intermediate
Finished block size: 11″ × 11″

Curvaceous Cabins, 66″ × 77″, made by Peggy J. Barkle

Throw a curve into a traditional Log Cabin quilt with this *Curvaceous Cabin*.

Materials

When choosing fabrics, think about the division the curve creates in the block. If you want the curve to be well defined, choose fabrics with a high contrast. If you want a softer transition, choose fabrics that have similar values. You will need 4 light fabrics and 4 dark fabrics as well as a center-square fabric.

¾ yard light fabric #1

1 yard light fabric #2

1½ yards light fabric #3

1⅝ yards light fabric #4

¾ yard dark fabric #1

1 yard dark fabric #2

1½ yards dark fabric #3

1⅝ yards dark fabric #4

¼ yard center-square fabric

⅞ yard bias-binding fabric for 2½″-wide double-fold binding

4¾ yards backing fabric (seam to run the length of grain)

72″ × 83″ batting

Cutting

Cut strips from selvage to selvage on the crosswise grain, unless otherwise noted.

1. From both the light and the dark fabrics #1, cut 11 strips 2″ wide (22 strips total).

2. From both the light and the dark fabrics #2, cut 15 strips 2″ wide (30 strips total).

3. From both the light and the dark fabrics #3, cut 24 strips 2″ wide (48 strips total).

4. From both the light and the dark fabrics #4, cut 27 strips 2″ wide (54 strips total).

5. Label these strips with their fabric numbers (#1, #2, #3, #4). These labels will help you determine the positions of the strips in the Log Cabin block.

6. From the center-square fabric, cut 2 strips 2″ wide.

Making the Blocks

The traditional Log Cabin piecing instructions are altered for this block to compensate for the distortion that will be created in the cutting and sewing of the curve.

The Log Cabin block is created from rectangular strips pieced around a center square and is traditionally constructed so that one side of the block is made from dark strips and the other from light strips. In this project, however, you will create entirely dark blocks and entirely light blocks, and the half-dark/half-light effect will be achieved by cutting the blocks apart with a gentle curve.

1. With right sides together, sew a strip of center-square fabric to 1 strip of dark fabric #1 and press the seam away from the center-square fabric. Subcut the strip into 21 segments 2″ wide.

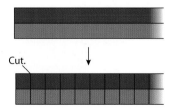

Cut.

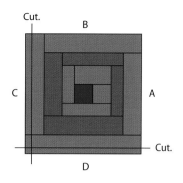

2. With rights sides together, chain piece the 21 units from Step 1 to strips of dark fabric #1 (join the sub-cuts along their longer side to the strips of dark fabric #1). Press the seams open. Subcut the strips into 21 segments.

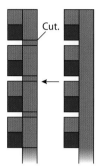

Cut.

3. Continue counterclockwise to add and subcut until the center square has been surrounded by fabric #1. Always press the seam open.

4. The blocks should measure 5″ × 5″ at this point. Use a 12½″ ruler to resize the blocks to 4½″ × 4½″ by trimming only the 2 sides with the longest strips (C and D).

Cut. B

C   A

Cut.

D

5. Repeat Steps 2–3 with fabric #2. Start by joining the blocks along side A to the strip of fabric #2. Square the blocks to 7″ × 7″ by trimming sides A and B, which are opposite the sides you trimmed last.

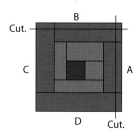

B

Cut.

C   A

D   Cut.

6. Repeat Steps 2–3 with fabric #3. Start by joining the blocks along side A to the strip of fabric #3. Square the blocks to 9½″ × 9½″ by trimming sides C and D, which are opposite the sides you trimmed last.

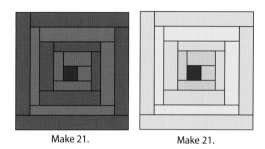

Cut.

B

C   A

Cut.

D

7. Repeat Steps 2–3 with fabric #4. Start by joining the blocks along side A to the strip of fabric #4. The blocks should measure 12½″ × 12½″. **Do not resize the blocks at this time.** You will have 21 dark blocks.

8. Construct the light-fabric blocks in the same manner described for the dark-fabric blocks. You will need 21 of each.

Make 21.   Make 21.

Cutting the Blocks

1. Pair half of the light blocks with half of the dark blocks **right sides up** in sets of 2, keeping the wide and skinny logs in the same orientation from one block to the next. Cut a gentle curve through the pairs and shuffle into new blocks. Remember that the abstract nature of this technique does not require you to match seam intersections.

2. Sew the halves of the new blocks together and press the seams open. Square the blocks to 11½″ × 11½″ by trimming the 2 sides opposite the sides you trimmed last. Squaring up the blocks after they have been cut and rejoined allows you to compensate for the distortion of the block created by the cutting and sewing process.

Stack, slice, shuffle, and sew.

Putting the Quilt Top Together

Refer to the Quilt Assembly Diagram (below) for quilt construction and to General Quilting Instructions (pages 104–109) as needed.

Arrange the blocks. Set the wider outside logs against the thinner logs of the neighboring block to add visual interest to the final design. Sew the blocks into rows. Sew the rows together, and press well. This quilt has no borders.

Quilt Assembly Diagram

Quilting and Finishing

Refer to pages 105–107 for quilting and finishing instructions.

1. Layer and baste the quilt. Quilt by hand or machine.

2. Finish the quilt.

notes on quilting

An allover quilting pattern is wonderful for this design. I used a pattern that incorporated both curves and points, but a pattern with soft curves or a rounded design will accentuate the curve of the pattern and be quite lovely. I matched the color of the thread closely to the color of the quilt so that the graphic design was not interrupted by the pattern or thread.

Free-form quilting design

autumn richness

Autumn Richness, 59½″ × 59½″, made by Lerlene Nevaril

Although this quilt uses only two blocks, the three different sashing colors and the pieced diamond border make it really vibrant. The diagonal motion created by the B blocks paired with the diamonds in the border creates a lot more movement than you would expect from a straight set.

Materials and Cutting

Fabric	Yardage	Used For	Number of Pieces	Cut Size
Green	1¼ yards	Block A, piece A	8	3½″ × 3½″
		Block B, piece A	8	3½″ × 3½″
		Sashing	12	2″ × 9½″
		Second border	12	Pattern A (page 74)
Green and Black Print	2 yards	Block A, piece B	32	2″ × 3½″
		Sashing	8	2″ × 9½″
		First border	5	2″ × fabric width
		Third border	6	5″ × fabric width
		Binding	6	2¼″ × fabric width
Rust	⅔ yard	Block A, piece D	32	2⅜″ × 2⅜″
		Block B, piece C	16	2⅜″ × 2⅜″
		Block A, piece E	32	2″ × 2″
		Block B, piece B	16	2″ × 2″
		Sashing squares	9	2″ × 2″
		First border corner squares	4	2″ × 2″
		Second border corner squares	4	4″ × 4″
		Third border corner squares	4	5″ × 5″
Brown	½ yard	Block A, piece C	32	2″ × 3½″
		Block A, piece F	16	2″ × 2″
		Block B, piece E	16	2″ × 2″
Gold	2½ yards	Block A, piece F	144	2″ × 2″
		Block A, piece G	32	2⅜″ × 2⅜″
		Block B, piece D	16	2⅜″ × 2⅜″
		Block B, piece F	16	3½″ × 3½″
		Block B, piece G	16	3½″ × 6½″
		Sashing	4	2″ × 9½″
		Second border	24	Pattern B (page 74)
		Second border	24	Pattern B reversed (page 74)
Backing	3¾ yards			
Batting	66″ × 66″			

Making the Blocks

BLOCK A

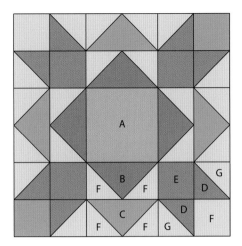

Make 8 blocks.

1. Use 32 rust D squares (2⅜″ × 2⅜″) and 32 gold G squares (2⅜″ × 2⅜″) to make 64 half-square triangle units (page 48).

Make 64 half-square triangle units.

2. Combine the half-square triangle units from Step 1 with 32 rust E Squares (2″ × 2″), and either 16 gold F squares (2″ × 2″) or 16 brown F squares (2″ × 2″), to make 16 units of each color combination.

Make 16 units of each.

3. Use 128 gold F squares (2″ × 2″), 32 brown print C rectangles (2″ × 3½″), and 32 green and black print rectangles (2″ × 3½″) to make 32 flying geese units in each color combination (page 108).

Sew and flip to make 32 of each.

4. Sew the Flying Geese units together to make 32 combined units.

Make 32 units.

5. Combine all the units with 8 green A squares (3½″ × 3½″) to make 8 blocks.

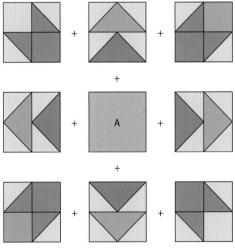

Make 8 blocks.

BLOCK B

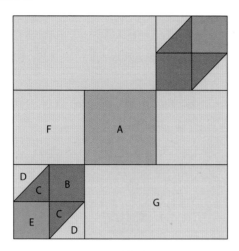

Make 8 blocks.

1. Use 16 rust C squares (2⅜″ × 2⅜″) and 16 gold D squares (2⅜″ × 2⅜″) to make 32 half-square triangle units (page 48).

Make 32 half-square triangle units.

2. Combine the half-square triangle units from Step 1 with 16 brown E squares (2″ × 2″) and 16 rust B squares (2″ × 2″) to make 16 units.

Make 16 units.

3. Combine 16 gold F squares (3½″ × 3½″) with 8 green A squares (3½″ × 3½″) to make 8 units.

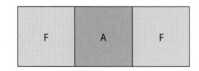

Make 8 units.

4. Combine the units from Step 2 with 16 gold G rectangles (3½″ × 6½″) to make 16 units.

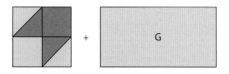

Make 16 units.

5. Sew all the units together to make 8 blocks.

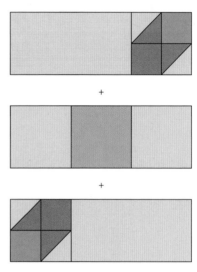

Make 8 blocks.

Putting the Quilt Top Together

Refer to the Quilt Assembly Diagram (next page) for quilt construction and to General Quilting Instructions (pages 104–109) as needed.

QUILT CENTER

1. Sew the blocks and sashings into horizontal rows. Press seams on odd rows to the left and even rows to the right.

2. Sew together rows of blocks and sashing strips to complete the quilt top. Press.

BORDERS

1. Add the borders one at a time, pressing toward the last border added.

2. Use the Border Assembly Diagram for the second border to sew four gold triangles to each green diamond. Press as you go. Piece four border strips of three diamond units each. Press. The patterns are on page 74.

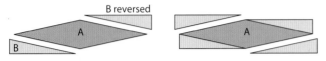

Border Assembly Diagram

Quilting and Finishing

Refer to pages 105–107 for quilting and finishing instructions.

1. Layer and baste the quilt. Quilt by hand or machine.

2. Finish the quilt.

piecing diamonds and triangles

Pieced diamonds and triangles in borders can be tricky to sew exactly. Follow these steps for success:

- Copy the template pattern, and glue it to template plastic.

- Cut out the plastic template along the solid lines.

- For ease in matching, punch a small hole where the seamlines (dashed lines) meet.

- Mark a dot on the wrong side of the fabric through the punched holes.

- When piecing and sewing the units together, match these marked dots.

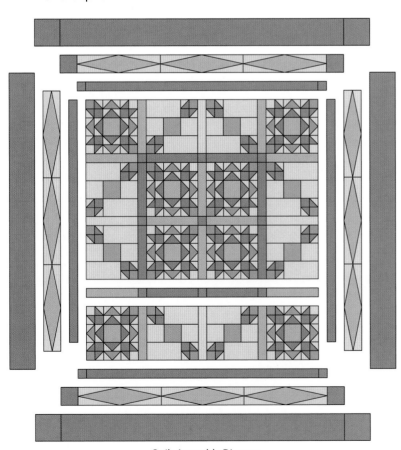

Quilt Assembly Diagram

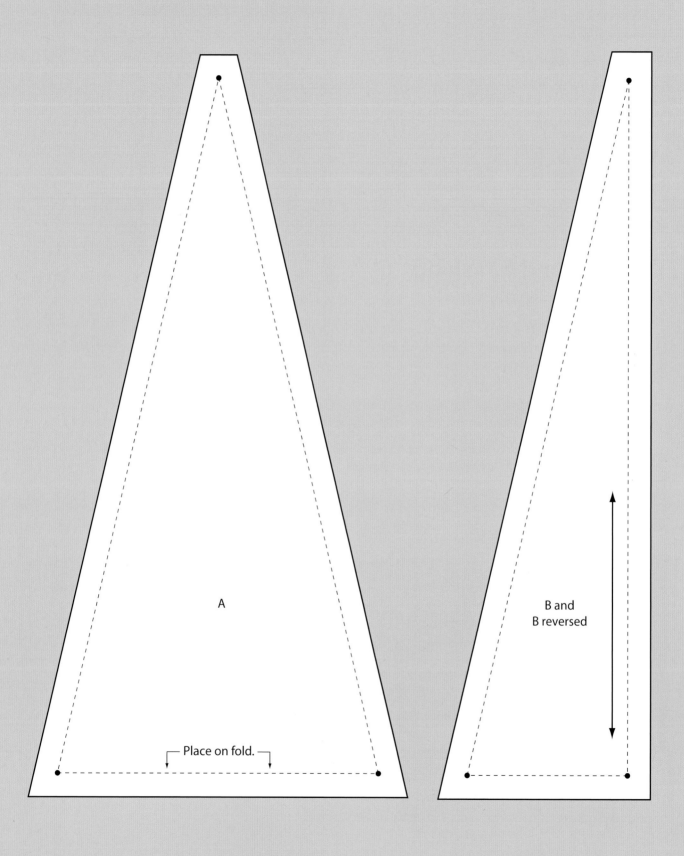

A

Place on fold.

B and
B reversed

pleiades pineapple

Challenging

Finished block size: 9″ × 9″

Finished Pineapple block size: 4⅝″ × 4⅝″

Pleiades Pineapple, 78½″ × 96½″, made by Dixie Haywood and Jane Hall, hand quilted by Sharon Steele
From the collection of Mary Underhill

This stunningly graphic design was created for the raffle quilt for the 1997 International Quilt Festival in Houston, Texas. It pays tribute to the Pleiades, a small cluster of stars in the constellation of Orion. You can create a wallhanging, or a smaller or larger quilt, by varying the number and size of blocks. It is easiest done by machine on paper or interfacing foundations, but can also be pieced by hand using fabric foundations.

Materials

Blue: 25 assorted fat quarters for the Pineapple blocks and Star block backgrounds

White-on-white: 16 assorted fat quarters for Pineapple blocks

Red: 9 assorted fat eighths for Star blocks

Red solid: ½ yard for inner border

Navy solid: ½ yard for middle border

Medium blue: 2 yards for outer border

Backing: 7 yards

Batting: 85″ × 103″

Binding: ⅝ yard

OTHER SUPPLIES

Paper-piecing foundation paper or lightweight removable interfacing for foundations

Pencil for tracing pattern

Cutting

PINEAPPLE BLOCKS

For each of the 9″ × 9″ blocks

Blue
Cut 4 strips 1¼″ × 22″.
Cut 2 squares 3″ × 3″, then cut once diagonally.
Cut 1 square 2″ × 2″.

White-on-white
Cut 4 strips 1¼″ × 18″.

For each of the 4½″ × 9″ half-blocks

Blue
Cut 2 strips 1¼″ × 22″.
Cut 1 square 3″ × 3″, then cut once diagonally.
Cut 1 rectangle 1¼″ × 2″.

White-on-white
Cut 2 strips 1¼″ × 18″.

For each of the 4½″ square quarter-blocks

Blue

Cut 1 square 1¼″ × 1¼″.

Cut 1 strip 1¼″ × 22″.

Cut 1 square 3″ × 3″, then cut once diagonally (you will only need one triangle).

White-on-white

Cut 2 strips 1¼″ × 18″.

STARS

Trace the Star block patterns on page 80 onto template plastic. For the nine 4⅝″ × 4⅝″ Star blocks, cut:

Red: 8 diamonds from each of the 9 fat eighths

Blue: 4 squares and 4 triangles each from 9 different blue fat quarters

BORDERS

Solid red: Cut 8 strips 1″ wide for the inner border.

Solid navy: Cut 8 strips 1½″ wide for the middle border.

Medium blue: Cut 9 strips 6½″ wide for the outer border.

Binding: Cut 10 strips 2″ wide by width of fabric.

Making the Blocks

PINEAPPLE BLOCK

1. Prepare the Pineapple foundations by enlarging the Pineapple pattern on page 80 200% so it is 9½″ × 9½″. Trace or copy 48 enlarged blocks onto paper-piecing foundation paper or lightweight removable interfacing. Trace 28 patterns for the half-blocks and 4 for the quarter-block patterns. To make patterns for the blocks with star insets, cut strips 10 and 11 from one corner of 12 foundations as shown.

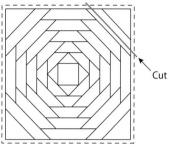

Make 12.

Cut strips 10 and 11 from two opposite corners of an additional 12 foundations as shown.

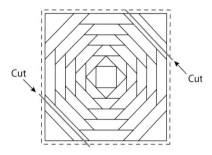

Make 12.

tip

If you choose a paper foundation, rather than tracing or copying multiple patterns, you can needlepunch the stitching lines by using an unthreaded sewing machine: Copy or trace 1 pattern. Stack up to 9 sheets underneath and use a long stitch length to make perforated stitching lines on the traced/printed lines. (If you feel that you will need the fabric placement lines, use a pencil to draw them in ¼″ beyond the stitching line.)

2. Pin or gluestick the blue center square onto the unmarked side of the foundation, right side up. Raw edges should overlap the stitching lines by ¼˝.

3. Cut 4 rectangles 2˝ long from the white strips (the finished size of the center square plus ¼˝ on each end). Pin the first white piece in place, right side down against the center square, matching the cut edges. Turn the unit over so the paper side is up and the fabric is against the feed dogs, and with a short stitch, sew on the line. Turn the unit over, finger-press the strip open, and pin it in place. Sew the second white strip to the opposite side of the square, pinning it in place on the right side and stitching on the paper side. Press. Follow this procedure to add white strips to the other two sides of the square. Press.

4. The second row of blue strips goes across the diagonal at the corners of the blue center square. Measure the finished length of the rectangle plus ¼˝ on each end. Cut 4 rectangles at this length from the first blue fabric strip. Sew opposite sides first, press, then add the 2 remaining opposite sides. Press.

5. As each row is completed, be sure to trim the seam allowances to ¼˝.

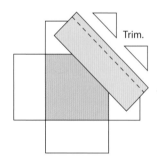

Trim.

tip

You can pin opposite sides and sew them without removing the foundation from the machine.

6. Continue to add white strips on the straight rows (odd-numbered) and blue strips on the diagonal rows (even-numbered).

7. Add the corner pieces (11) as indicated on the foundation.

8. After completing the 48 full blocks (including those with strips 10/11 removed), make the 28 half-blocks and the 4 quarter-blocks in the same fashion.

STAR BLOCK

1. Sew red diamonds into pairs, stopping ¼˝ from outside edge. Backstitch.

2. Inset the corner squares using Y-seam construction. **NOTE:** For additional help in this technique, go to www.ctpub.com > Consumer Resources > Quiltmaking Basics: Tips & Techniques for Quiltmaking & More > Y-Seam Construction.

3. Sew the pairs to one another and inset side triangles.

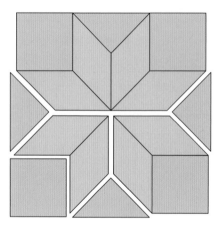

Star block—Make 12.

Putting the Quilt Top Together

Refer to the Quilt Assembly Diagram (next page) for quilt construction and to General Quilting Instructions (pages 104–109) as needed.

1. Sew the blue-and-white Pineapple blocks into rows, using the outside solid line of the foundation as a stitching guide. Use Y-seam construction to set in the Star blocks to the row above, as each row is constructed.

2. Join rows together. Set in the Star blocks to the row below as each row is joined to the one above.

3. Join the red inner border strips end to end to make one long strip. Do the same with the middle and outer border strips.

4. With foundations still in place to prevent stretching of the quilt top, measure and cut to length the side inner borders (page 104), and sew them to the quilt top.
Do the same for the top and bottom borders. Press toward the borders.

5. In a similar manner, add the side middle borders, then the top and bottom middle borders. Press.

6. Add the side outer borders, then the top and bottom outer borders. Press.

7. Carefully remove the foundation material from all the blocks.

Star block positioned for setting in.

Quilt Assembly Diagram

Quilting and Finishing

Refer to pages 105–107 for quilting and finishing instructions.

1. Layer and baste the quilt. Quilt by hand or machine.

2. Finish the quilt.

Pineapple foundation pattern. Enlarge 200%. Make 63.

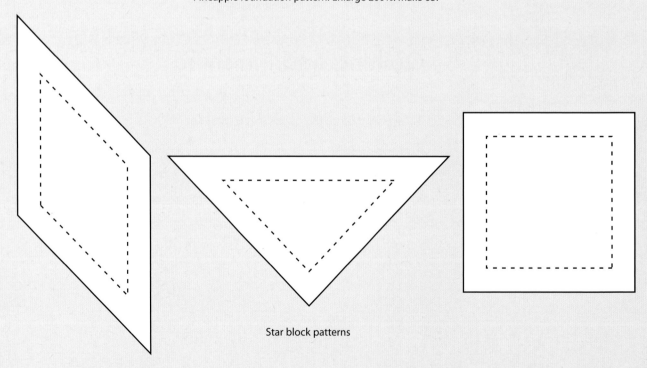

Star block patterns

tropical butterflies

Tropical Butterflies, 73″ × 89½″, made by Pam Stallebrass, machine quilted by Beverley Patterson, and hand quilted by Pat Thorne

Let your imagination take flight, and choose your favorite motif for this striking quilt. For the center blocks you can fussy-cut a print, create an appliqué, use a rubber stamp or a stencil—the choice is yours.

Materials

¾ yard of plain fabric for stamped or appliquéd block centers or more as needed to fussy-cut print centers

¼ yard each of 12 fabrics in warm and bright tones of gold, terra-cotta, orange, red, maroon, and purple for the blocks

4¾ yards of black for the blocks and sashing

¾ yard of red-orange for the inner border

2⅓ yards of black for the outer border

¾ yard of maroon for binding

Batting: 77″ × 93″

Backing: 77″ × 93″

Cutting

Block centers

Cut 12 squares 6½″ × 6½″.

Warm and bright colors

Cut 12 strips 1⅜″ × the fabric width for the colored frames around the butterflies. From the strips, cut 4 pieces for each block, 2 each of 7″ and 9″ lengths. These pieces are cut oversize for paper piecing.

Cut 20 squares 1½″ × 1½″ for the sashing squares.

Cut 12 strips 3½″ × the fabric width, then cut into squares 3½″ × 3½″. Cut in half diagonally to make half-square triangles. Each block needs 16, for a total of 192. Cut a few extra. These pieces are cut oversize for paper piecing.

Black

Cut 68 strips 2″ × the fabric width for the Log Cabin strips. From the strips, cut 16 pieces for each block, 4 each of 8½″, 10½″, 12½″, and 14½″ lengths. These pieces are cut oversize for paper piecing.

Cut 16 strips 1½″ × the fabric width, then cut into 1½″ × 16″ pieces for sashing. Cut 31 pieces.

Cut 8 strips 9″ × the fabric width for the outer border.

Red-orange

Cut 7 strips 3″ × the fabric width for the inner border.

Making the Blocks

1. For each block, trace or photocopy the pattern (page 85) 4 times, then tape the copies together to make a 15½˝ block. Add a ¼˝ seam allowance around the outside edge. Add the numbers, as they show the order to add the fabric pieces. Draw seamlines in the corners of the center block frame (pieces 2–5). Make 12 patterns.

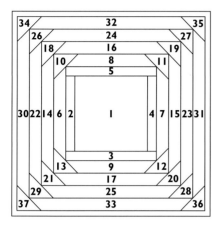

Paper-piecing pattern

2. Place the paper foundation on a light table (or up against a window) and carefully center the center block design on the blank side. Pin in place.

Center and pin.

3. Select one of the 1⅜˝ × 7˝ strips for the frame. Align it with the #2 strip on the pattern, and pin in place. With the right side of the paper up, stitch on the line between #1 and #2. Press open. Trim off the excess strip.

Pin frame strip.

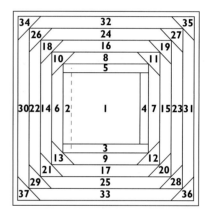

Stitch.

Press open.

4. Repeat for pieces #3–#5.

5. Take the 2″ black strips and sew them in place (pieces #6–#9).

6. Take 4 triangles of the same color and add these next (pieces #10–#13).

7. Repeat Steps 5 and 6 with the longer black strips and different colored triangles to complete the block. Carefully tear away the paper from each block.

8. Trim each block to 16″ × 16″.

Putting the Quilt Top Together

Refer to the Quilt Assembly Diagram (to the right) for quilt construction and to General Quilting Instructions (pages 104–109) as needed.

1. Arrange and join the blocks and sashing.

2. Trim the selvages from the inner border strips and sew into 1 long length.

3. Measure the quilt top from top to bottom through the center, and cut 2 inner border strips this length. Add to the sides of the quilt top, and press.

4. Measure the quilt top from side to side through the center and cut 2 inner border strips this length. Add to the top and bottom of the quilt top and press.

5. Repeat Steps 2–4 to join, measure, cut, and add the outer borders.

Quilting and Finishing

Refer to pages 105–107 for quilting and finishing instructions.

1. Layer and baste the quilt. Quilt by hand or machine.

2. Finish the quilt.

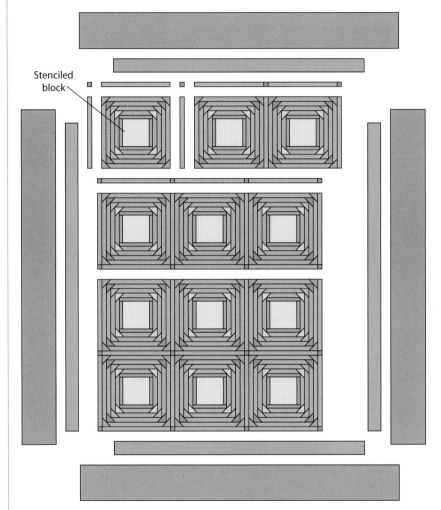

Stenciled block

Quilt Assembly Diagram

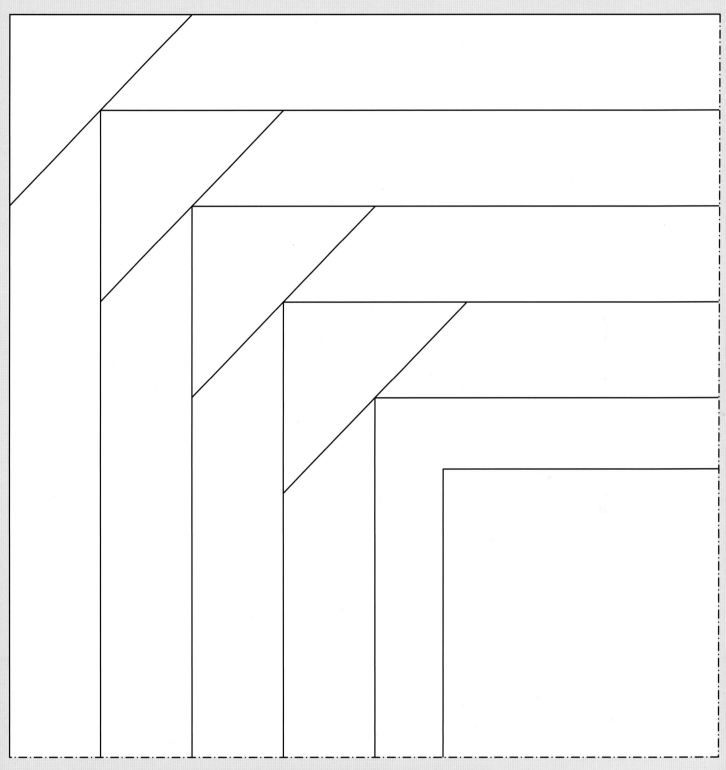

Quarter of foundation—copy 4 and tape together.

coming storms

□□□□
Challenging
Finished block size: 14″ × 14″

Coming Storms, 58½″ × 72½″, designed by Margrit Hall, made by Cathryn Tallman-Evans, quilted by Phyllis Reddish

Inspired by the sea, this quilt combines the traditional Storm at Sea and Mariner's Compass into a nautical-themed beauty.

Materials and Cutting

Patterns for triangles A and B and paper-pieced Mariner's Compass block and Corner block are on pages 91–92.

Fabric Color	Fabric Amount	Cutting Directions
Light Blue Background	2⅛ yards	Cut 2 strips 3⅜″ wide, then cut into 24 squares 3⅜″ × 3⅜″. Cut each square once on the diagonal to make 48 triangles.
		Cut 8 strips 4″ wide. Stack strips with wrong sides together and cut 96 pairs of A's (96 A and 96 A reverse).
		Cut 6 strips 2⅛″ wide, then cut into 96 squares 2⅛″ × 2⅛″. Cut each square once on the diagonal to make 192 triangles.
		Cut 2 strips 2″ wide, then cut into 32 rectangles 2″ × 2½″. Set aside for paper-pieced Mariner's Compass corner block.
		Cut 3 strips 3″ wide, then cut into 32 squares 3″ × 3″. Set aside for paper-pieced Mariner's Compass corner block.
Blue & Green Wave	1¾ yards	Cut 2 strips 4″ wide, then cut into 12 squares 4″ × 4″. Cut 7 strips 6½″ wide. Set aside for 3rd border.
Dark Blue Swirl	1 yard	Cut 3 strips 4⅜″ wide, then cut into 24 squares 4⅜″ × 4⅜″. Cut each square on the diagonal to make 48 triangles.
		Cut 6 strips 2″ wide. Set aside for 1st border.
Purple Multicolor	⅞ yard	Cut 6 strips 4″ wide, then cut into 96 B's.
Dark Turquoise	⅝ yard	Cut 7 strips 2⅝″ wide, then cut into 96 squares 2⅝″ × 2⅝″. Cut each square once on the diagonal to make 192 triangles.
Light Turquoise	⅝ yard	Cut 3 strips 2¼″ wide, then cut into 48 squares 2¼″ × 2¼″. Cut 7 strips 1¼″ wide. Set aside for 2nd border.
Dark Purple Solid	½ yard	Cut 1 strip 2½″ wide, then cut into 4 rectangles 7″ × 2½″. Set aside for paper-pieced center Mariner's Compass block.
		Cut 1 strip 4″ wide, then cut into 16 rectangles 4″ × 1½″. Set aside for paper-pieced Mariner's Compass corner block.
Light Purple Solid	½ yard	Cut 1 strip 2½″ wide, then cut into 4 rectangles 7″ × 2½″. Set aside for paper-pieced center Mariner's Compass block.
		Cut 1 strip 4″ wide, then cut into 16 rectangles 4″ × 1½″. Set aside for paper-pieced Mariner's Compass corner block.
Dark Green Solid	⅜ yard	Cut 1 strip 2″ wide, then cut into 4 rectangles 5½″ × 2″. Set aside for paper-pieced center Mariner's Compass block.
		Cut 1 strip 3½″ wide, then cut into 16 rectangles 3½″ × 1″. Set aside for paper-pieced Mariner's Compass corner block.
Light Green Solid	⅜ yard	Cut 1 strip 2″ wide, then cut into 4 rectangles 5½″ × 2″. Set aside for paper-pieced center Mariner's Compass block.
		Cut 1 strip 3½″ wide, then cut into 16 rectangles 3½″ × 1¼″. Set aside for paper-pieced Mariner's Compass corner block.
Dark Orange Solid	¼ yard	Cut 1 strip 1¼″ wide, then cut into 8 rectangles 1¼″ × 4½″. Set aside for paper-pieced center Mariner's Compass block.
		Cut 1 strip 2¼″ wide, then cut into 32 rectangles 2¼″ × 1″. Set aside for paper-pieced Mariner's Compass corner block.
Light Orange Solid	¼ yard	Cut 1 strip 1¼″ wide, then cut into 8 rectangles 1¼″ × 4½″. Set aside for paper-pieced center Mariner's Compass block.
		Cut 1 strip 2¼″ wide, then cut into 32 rectangles 2¼″ × 1″. Set aside for paper-pieced Mariner's Compass corner block.
Dark Teal	⅝ yard	Cut 8 strips 2¼″ wide for binding.
Backing	3⅝ yards	Piece horizontally.

Making the Blocks

Press the seams in the direction of the arrows, unless otherwise indicated.

1. Sew 3⅜″ light blue background triangles to opposite sides of a blue and green 4″ × 4″ square. Press. Sew 3⅜″ background triangles to the remaining sides of the 4″ × 4″ blue and green square to make Unit A. Press. Make 12 Unit A's.

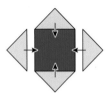

Unit A—Make 12.

2. Sew 4⅜″ dark blue triangles to opposite sides of Unit A. Press. Sew 4⅜″ dark blue triangles to the remaining sides of Unit A to make Section 1. Press. Make 12 Section 1's.

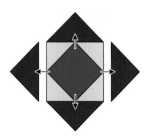

Section 1—Make 12.

3. Sew a background A triangle to the right side and a background A reverse triangle to the left side of a purple B triangle to make Unit B. Press. Make 96 Unit B's.

Unit B—Make 96.

4. Sew 2 Unit B's together to make Section 2. Press. Make 48 Section 2's.

Section 2—Make 48.

5. Sew 2⅛″ background triangles to opposite sides of a light turquoise 2¼″ × 2¼″ square. Press. Sew 2⅛″ background triangles to the remaining sides of the square to make Unit C. Press. Make 48 Unit C's.

Unit C—Make 48.

6. Sew 2⅝″ dark turquoise triangles to opposite sides of Unit C. Press. Sew 2⅝″ dark turquoise triangles to the remaining sides of Unit C to make Section 3. Make 48 Section 3's.

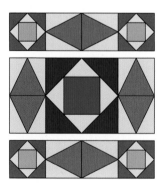

Section 3—Make 48.

7. Sew the sections together to make a complete block. Press seams open. Make 12 blocks.

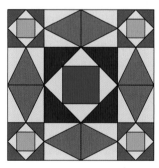

Complete block—Make 12.

Putting the Quilt Top Together

Refer to the Quilt Assembly Diagram (page 90) for quilt construction and to General Quilting Instructions (pages 104–109) as needed.

1. Sew 3 blocks together for each row. Press seams open.

2. Sew the rows together to make the quilt body. Press seams open.

FIRST BORDER

Before cutting all final borders, measure your quilt top to confirm measurements for the strip lengths.

1. Sew 2″-wide dark blue strips end-to-end as necessary and cut 2 border strips 42½″ long. Sew to the top and bottom of the quilt and press.

2. Sew 2″-wide dark blue strips end-to-end as necessary and cut 2 border strips 59½″ long. Sew to the sides of the quilt and press.

SECOND BORDER

1. Sew 1¼″-wide light turquoise strips end-to-end as necessary and cut 2 border strips 45½″ long. Sew to the top and bottom of the quilt and press.

2. Sew 1¼″-wide light turquoise strips end-to-end as necessary and cut 2 border strips 61″ long. Sew to the sides of the quilt and press.

CORNER BLOCK ASSEMBLY

Refer to General Quilting Instructions on pages 108–109 for paper-piecing instructions.

1. Using the precut rectangles and squares, paper-piece Section A and Section B of the corner blocks. Make 16 of each section.

Section A—Make 16.

Section B—Make 16.

2. Sew a Section A to a Section B to make one-quarter of the corner block. Press seam open. Make 8.

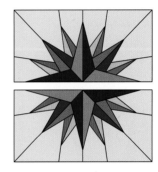

One-quarter block—Make 8.

3. Sew quarters into halves, and then sew 2 halves together to make a corner block. Make 4 corner blocks. Trim to a 6½″ × 6½″ square. Press seam open. Remove the paper.

Make 4 corner blocks.

THIRD BORDER

1. Sew 6½″-wide blue and green strips end-to-end as necessary and cut 2 border strips 47″ long. Sew to the top and bottom of the quilt and press.

2. Sew 6½″-wide blue and green strips end-to-end as necessary and cut 2 border strips 61″ long.

3. Sew corner blocks to both ends of each side strip. Press. Sew to the sides of the quilt and press.

CENTER MARINER'S COMPASS APPLIQUÉ

1. Using the precut rectangles and squares, paper-piece Sections A and B of the center Mariner's Compass block. Sew to the dots and backstitch. Do not sew through the ¼″ seam allowance. Make 4 of each section.

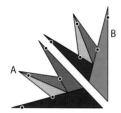

2. Sew A and B together to make one-quarter of the block. Sew to the dots and backstitch. Do not sew through the ¼" seam allowance.

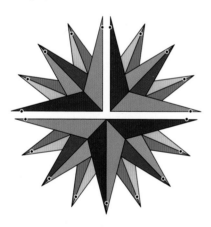

One-quarter of block—Make 4.

3. Sew quarters into halves, and then sew 2 halves together to make the block. Sew to the dots and backstitch. Do not sew through the ¼" seam allowance. Trim and remove the paper.

Completing Mariner's Compass block

4. Mark and turn under ¼" seam allowances around the edges of the block. Press edges under and appliqué to the quilt. Use the quilt photo on page 86 for placement.

Quilting and Finishing

Refer to pages 105–107 for quilting and finishing instructions.

1. Layer and baste the quilt. Quilt by hand or machine.

2. Finish the quilt.

Quilt Assembly Diagram

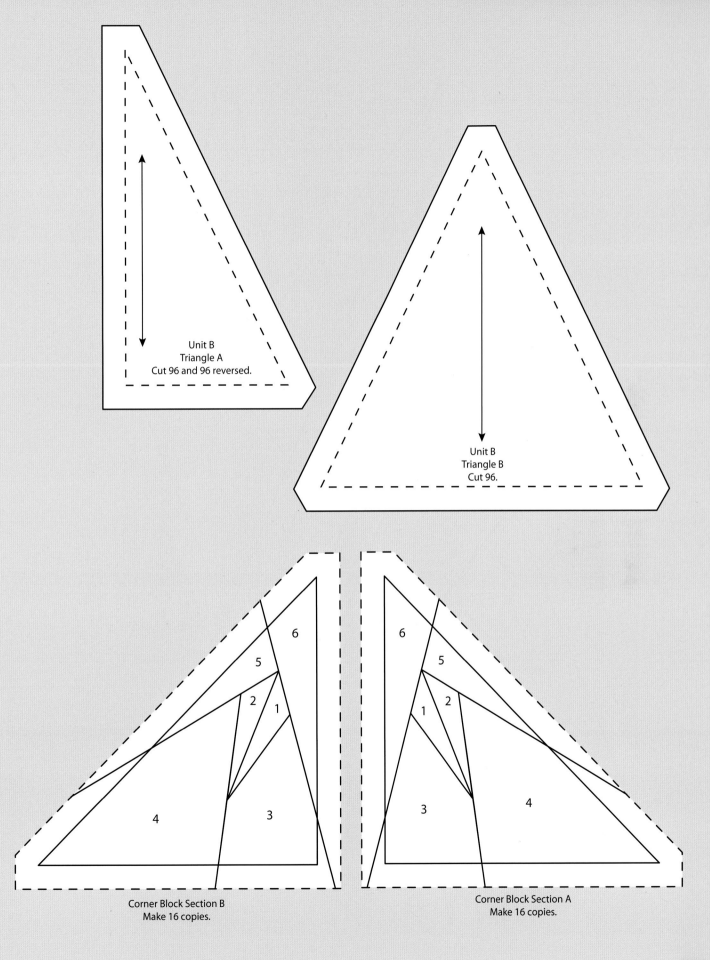

Unit B
Triangle A
Cut 96 and 96 reversed.

Unit B
Triangle B
Cut 96.

Corner Block Section B
Make 16 copies.

Corner Block Section A
Make 16 copies.

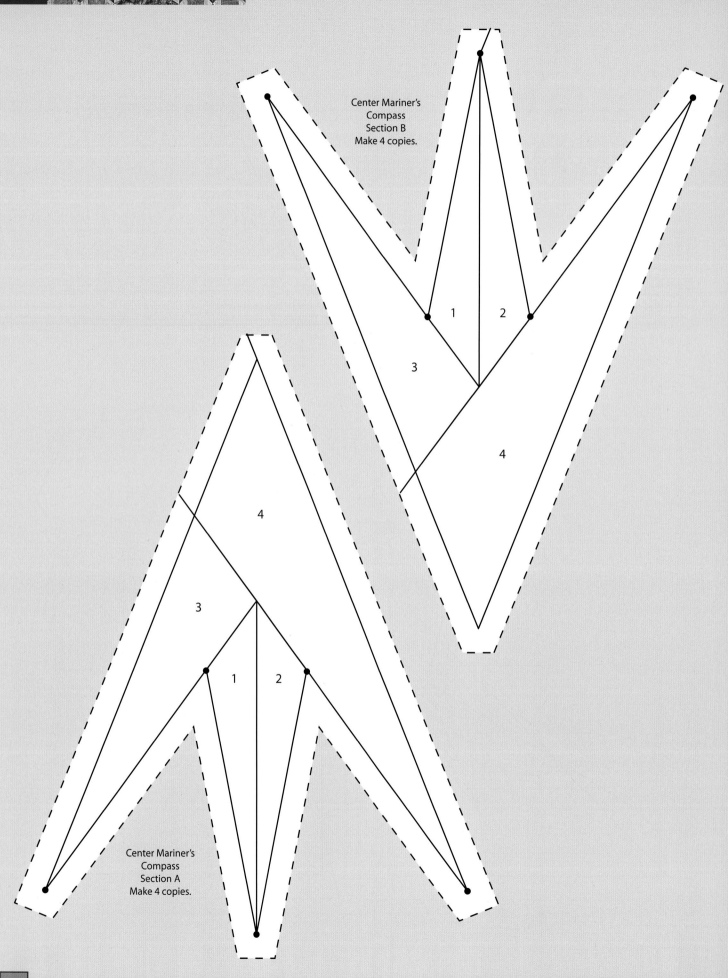

Center Mariner's
Compass
Section B
Make 4 copies.

Center Mariner's
Compass
Section A
Make 4 copies.

bow tie medley

Bow Tie Medley, 71″ × 71″, made by Rebecca Wat

Yes, it looks just like the traditional Bow Tie block. But when you touch this block or look at it at an angle, you immediately notice the dimension and unique texture—one that even allows you to run your fingers underneath. This is a very different Bow Tie block, a brand-new fabric origami block. For this quilt, what you have to make sure of is that you have enough different fabrics. By the way, it is fun to match up Bow Ties with background fabrics— a process similar to finding the right shirt for a tie and vice versa.

Materials

Bow ties: 20 or more fabrics to total 4 yards

Contrasting fabrics: 20 or more fabrics to total 2 yards

Background: 3 yards

Backing: 4¼ yards

Binding: 2 yards for lengthwise cut OR ⅞ yard for crosswise cut

Batting: 75″ × 75″

Cutting

Bow ties: Cut 116 squares 6½″ × 6½″.

Contrasting fabrics: Cut 232 squares 3¼″ × 3¼″. (Cut pairs of squares from the same fabric for each block.)

Background and sashing:

Cut 29 squares 5″ × 5″.

Cut 162 rectangles 1″ × 5″.

Cut 22 strips 1″ × the width of the fabric.

Cut 8 squares 9⅛″ × 9⅛″. Cut each square diagonally twice for side triangles.

Cut 2 squares 4⅞″ × 4⅞″. Cut each square diagonally once for corner triangles.

Binding: Cut strips 3¼″ wide lengthwise or crosswise to total 296″ after piecing the strips end to end.

Folding

For step-by-step photos and guidelines, refer to Bow Tie Folding Instructions, Steps 1–24, on pages 96–99.

Hint: To save time, do each of the following steps by batch.

1. Follow the folding instructions Steps 1–11 (pages 96–97) to fold the 6½″ squares into 116 folded squares.

2. Follow the folding instructions Steps 12–15 (page 97–98) to stitch the folded squares.

3. Open the folded squares and press, according to the folding instructions Steps 16–18 (page 98). Each folded square should measure 5″ × 5″.

4. Tuck a pair of 3¼″ squares under each folded bow, as shown in the folding instructions Steps 19–20 (page 99).

5. Sew the 3¼″ squares in place, as shown in the folding instructions Steps 21–24 (page 99).

Putting the Quilt Top Together

Refer to the Quilt Assembly Diagram (to the right) for quilt construction and to General Quilting Instructions (pages 104–109) as needed.

1. Arrange all the pieces.

2. Sew together by diagonal row the Bow Tie blocks, background blocks, short sashing pieces, and side triangles. Press toward the sashing.

3. Piece the 1″-wide sashing strips together end to end as necessary.

4. Sew the rows together.

5. Use a quilting ruler and rotary cutter to square the quilt. Trim the side triangles.

Quilting and Finishing

Refer to pages 105–107 for quilting and finishing instructions.

1. Layer and baste the quilt. Quilt by hand or machine.

2. Finish the quilt.

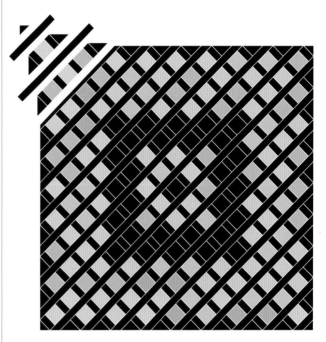

Quilt Assembly Diagram

Bow Tie Folding Instructions

1. Place the fabric right side up and fold the square in half. Finger-press. Repeat in the opposite direction to form an intersection of creases.

2. Turn over the square so the wrong side is up. These are the creases you'll pick up in Steps 3–9.

3. Pick up the left half of the horizontal crease and align it with the top left corner.

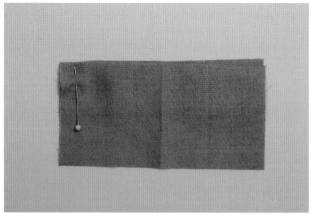

4. Pin the crease to the top left corner.

5. Rotate the fabric one-quarter turn to the right. Pick up the left half of the horizontal crease and align it with the top left corner.

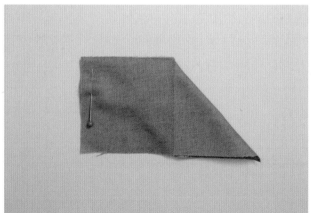

6. Pin the crease to the top left corner.

7. Rotate the fabric one-quarter turn to the right. Pick up the left half of the horizontal crease and align it with the top left corner.

8. Pin the crease to the top left corner.

9. Rotate the fabric one-quarter turn to the right. Pick up the left half of the horizontal crease and align it with the top left corner.

10. Pin the crease to the top left corner. A puff is formed at the center.

11. Press the puff to form a diamond shape. Remove the pins and iron-press.

12. Insert a threaded needle in the center of one side of the diamond to pick up a little bit of fabric.

13. Repeat Step 12 on the remaining 3 sides.

14. Return to where you first started sewing.

15. Pull the thread to gather all the sides to the center. Make a knot and cut the thread.

16. Spread out the fabric to its full extent to form a square.

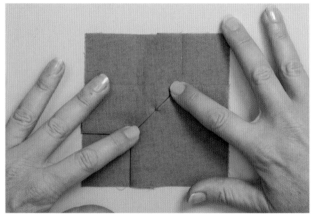

17. Arrange the pleats as shown.

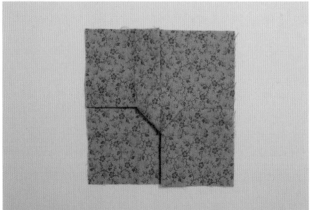

18. Turn over the fabric and iron-press. You can now piece this as a regular quilt block.

19. For variation, place a piece of lace or contrasting fabric under the bow.

20. Repeat Step 19 on the other side.

21. Fold the block in half.

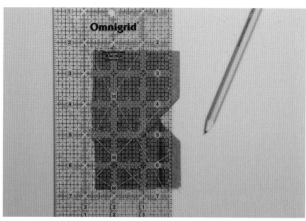

22. Sew with a ¼″ seam allowance, catching the lace or contrasting fabric in the seam.

23. Cut off the excess thread. Repeat Step 22 on the other side to secure the lace or fabric under the Bow Tie.

24. You can now piece this as a regular quilt block.

scrappy triangles

□□□□
Challenging

Finished block size: 4½″ × 4½″

Scrappy Triangles, 67″ × 68½″, made by Alex Anderson

This scrappy quilt is pieced using two Nine-Patch variations. The instructions tell you how many individual half-square triangles to cut, but you can substitute your favorite quick-piecing method to make scrappy half-square triangle units. The floral appliqué border makes this quilt a beauty.

Materials

Assorted cream prints: 3 yards total for blocks, extra row, and outer border

Assorted dark red prints: 1¾ yards total for blocks, extra row, and pieced binding

Assorted medium and dark prints: 1⅝ yards total for blocks and extra row

Beige and cream stripe: ½ yard for inner border

Dark green print: 1¼ yards for vine and leaf appliqués

Assorted print scraps: 1½ yards total for flower and berry appliqués

Batting: 71″ × 73″

Backing: 4 yards

Cutting

Assorted cream prints

Cut a total of 281 squares 2⅜″ × 2⅜″, then cut in half diagonally. You'll need 561 triangles for the blocks and extra row. (You'll have 1 triangle left over.)

Cut 7½″-wide strips to total 250″ for the pieced outer border.

Assorted dark red prints

Cut a total of 281 squares 2⅜″ × 2⅜″, then cut in half diagonally. You'll need 561 triangles for the blocks and extra row. (You'll have 1 triangle left over.)

Cut a total of 7 strips 2⅛″ × the fabric width for the pieced binding.

Assorted medium and dark prints

Cut a total of 561 squares 2″ × 2″ for the blocks and extra row.

Beige and cream stripe

Cut 6 strips 2″ × the fabric width for the inner border.

Dark green print

Cut 1″-wide bias strips to total 300″ for the appliqué vine.

Cut 92 of A using the pattern on page 103 for the appliqué leaves.

Assorted print scraps

Cut 36 each of B, C, and D; 24 each of E and F; and 52 of G using the patterns on page 103 for the flower and berry appliqués.

Making the Blocks

Press in the direction of the arrows.

SCRAPPY TRIANGLE BLOCKS

You'll need a total of 121 Scrappy Triangle blocks: 61 Block A and 60 Block B.

1. Stitch assorted cream print and dark red print triangles in pairs; press. Make 561.

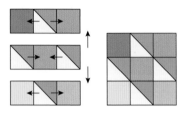

2. Arrange 4 units from Step 1 then 5 assorted medium and dark print 2″ squares in 3 rows as shown. Stitch the units and squares into rows; press. Stitch the rows together; press. Make 61.

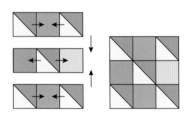

Block A

3. Arrange 5 units from Step 1 then 4 assorted medium and dark print 2″ squares in 3 rows as shown. Stitch the units and squares into rows; press. Stitch the rows together; press. Make 60.

Block B

Putting the Quilt Top Together

Refer to the Quilt Assembly Diagram (next page) for quilt construction and to General Quilting Instructions (pages 104–109) as needed.

QUILT CENTER

1. Lay out the 121 Scrappy Triangle blocks, alternating Block A and Block B as shown in the Quilt Assembly Diagram (next page). Stitch the blocks into rows; press.

2. Alternate the remaining units from Scrappy Triangle blocks with the remaining 2″ assorted dark and medium print squares to make the extra row along the bottom edge of the blocks. Press.

3. Stitch the rows together; press. Your quilt should measure 50″ × 51½″.

ADDING THE BORDERS

1. Join the 2″-wide beige and cream stripe strips end to end. (Since you are working with a striped fabric, you may prefer not to angle these seams.) Refer to Partial-Seam Borders (next page) to trim and sew the inner borders to the quilt top.

2. Stitch the 7½″-wide cream print strips end to end to make a pieced border strip approximately 250″ long. (You can piece these borders with straight seams as well.) Refer to Partial-Seam Borders to trim 4 outer border strips to the necessary lengths.

3. Appliqué 8 lengths of vine and pieces A–G to the outer borders. Refer to the quilt photo (page 100) to help with placement (template patterns are on page 103). Leave enough unattached vine to complete the corners. You'll cover the ends of each corner vine with a flower once the border is stitched to the quilt top.

4. Use the partial-seam technique to sew the appliquéd borders to the quilt top. Finish stitching the corner appliqué; press.

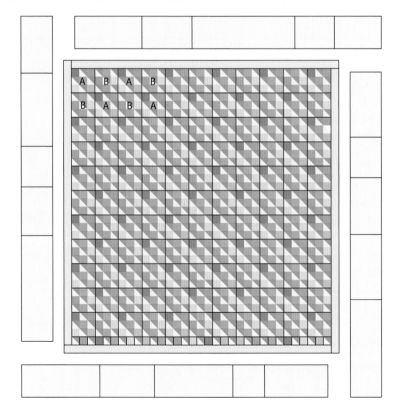

Quilt Assembly Diagram (border appliqué not shown)

SPECIAL TECHNIQUES

Partial-Seam Borders

1. Measure your quilt from top to bottom through the center of the quilt. Add the finished width of the border plus ½" (for seam allowances) to this measurement, and cut the side borders to this length.

2. Measure your quilt from side to to through the center of the quilt. Add the finished width of the border plus ½" (for seam allowances) to this measurement, and cut the top and bottom borders to this length.

3. Start on the side (as shown), and pin a side border strip to the quilt so that it extends past the bottom edge of the quilt by the finished width of the border plus ½".

4. Start at the top edge, and sew the side border strip #1 to the quilt top stopping 3" from the bottom corner of the quilt.

5. Sew border strips #2, #3, and #4 to the quilt.

6. You can now finish stitching the partially sewn seam.

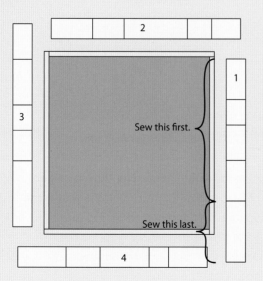

Quilting and Finishing

Refer to pages 105–107 for quilting and finishing instructions.

1. Layer and baste the quilt. Quilt by hand or machine.

2. Finish the quilt.

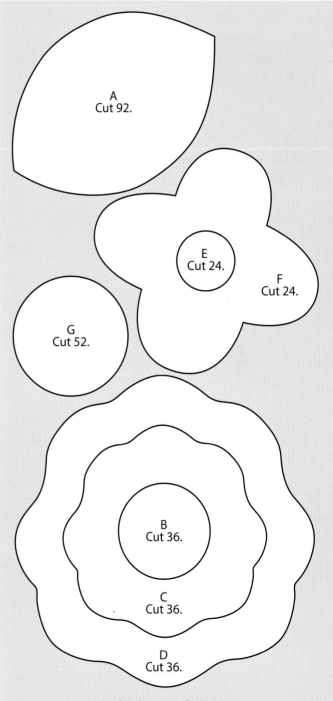

Appliqué patterns for border.
Patterns do not include seam allowance.

General QUILTING Instructions

Basic Guidelines

SEAM ALLOWANCES

A ¼˝ seam allowance is used for most projects. It's a good idea to do a test seam before you begin sewing to check that your ¼˝ is accurate. Accuracy is the key to successful piecing.

PRESSING

In general, press seams toward the darker fabric. Press lightly in an up-and-down motion. Avoid using a very hot iron or over-ironing, which can distort shapes and blocks.

BORDERS

When border strips are to be cut on the crosswise grain, diagonally piece the strips together to achieve the needed lengths.

Butted Borders

In most cases the side borders are sewn on first. When you have finished the quilt top, measure it through the center vertically. This will be the length to cut the side borders. Place pins at the centers of all four sides of the quilt top, as well as in the center of each side border strip. Pin the side borders to the quilt top first, matching the center pins. Using a ¼˝ seam allowance, sew the borders to the quilt top, and press toward the border.

Measure horizontally across the center of the quilt top, including the side borders. This will be the length to cut the top and bottom borders. Repeat pinning, sewing, and pressing.

Mitered Corner Borders

Measure the length of the quilt top and add two times the cut width of your border, plus 5˝. This is the length you need to cut or piece the side borders.

Place pins at the centers of both side borders and all four sides of the quilt top. From the center pin, measure in both directions and mark half of the measured length of the quilt top on both side borders. Pin, matching centers and the marked length of the side border to the edges of the quilt top. Stitch the strips to the sides of the quilt top by starting ¼˝ in from the beginning of the border seam, backstitching, and then continuing down the length of the side border. Stop stitching ¼˝ before the edge of the quilt top at the seam allowance line, and backstitch. The excess length of the side borders will extend beyond each edge. Press seams toward the border.

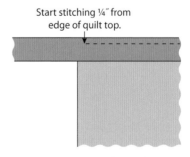

Start stitching ¼˝ from edge of quilt top.

Stop stitching ¼˝ from edge.

Determine the length needed for the top and bottom border in the same way, measuring the width of the quilt top through the center, including each side border. Add two times the cut width of your border plus 5˝ to this measurement. Cut or piece these border strips to this length. From the center of each border strip, measure in both directions, and mark half of the measured width of the quilt top. Again, pin, and then stitch up to the previous stitching line, and backstitch. The border strips extend beyond each end.

To create the miter, lay the corner on the ironing board. Working with the quilt right side up, lay one border strip on top of the adjacent border.

Press the top border seam allowance toward the border. With right sides up, fold the top border strip under itself so that it meets the edge of the adjacent border and forms a 45° angle. Pin the fold in place.

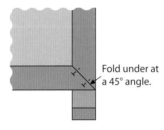

Fold under at a 45° angle.

Position a 90° angle triangle or ruler over the corner to check that the corner is flat and square. When everything is in place, press the fold firmly.

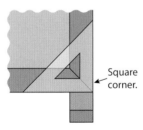

Square corner.

Remove pins. Fold the center section of the top diagonally from the corner, right sides together, and align the long edges of the border strips. On the wrong side, place pins near the pressed fold in the corner to secure the border strips.

Beginning at the inside corner at the border seamline, stitch, backstitch, and then stitch along the fold toward the outside point of the border corners, being careful not to allow any stretching to occur. Backstitch at the end. Trim the excess border fabric to ¼" seam allowance. Press the seam open.

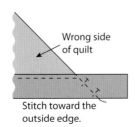

Wrong side of quilt

Stitch toward the outside edge.

BACKING

Plan on making the backing a minimum of 8" longer and wider than the quilt top. Piece, if necessary. Trim the selvages before you piece to the desired size.

To economize, you can piece the back from any leftover quilting fabrics or blocks in your collection.

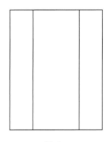

Twin

Full or Double

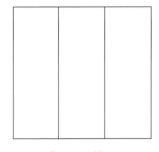

Queen or King

BATTING

The type of batting to use is a personal decision; consult your local quilt shop. Cut batting approximately 8" longer and wider than your quilt top.

LAYERING

Spread the backing wrong side up and tape the edges down with masking tape. (If you are working on carpet, you can use T-pins to secure the backing to the carpet.) Center the batting on top, smoothing out any folds. Place the quilt top right side up on top of the batting and backing, making sure it is centered.

BASTING

If you plan to machine quilt, pin-baste the quilt layers together with safety pins placed a minimum of 3″–4″ apart. Begin basting in the center and move toward the edges first in vertical, then horizontal, rows.

If you plan to hand quilt, baste the layers together with thread using a long needle and light-colored thread. Knot one end of the thread. Using stitches approximately the length of the needle, begin in the center and move out toward the edges in vertical and horizontal rows approximately 4″ apart. Add 2 diagonal rows of basting.

QUILTING

Quilting, whether by hand or machine, enhances the pieced or appliquéd design of the quilt. You may choose to quilt in-the-ditch, echo the pieced or appliqué motifs, use patterns from quilting design books and stencils, or do your own free-motion quilting. Suggested quilting patterns are included in some of the projects.

BINDING

Trim excess batting and backing from the quilt.

Double-Fold Straight-Grain Binding (French Fold)

If you want a ¼″ finished binding, cut the binding strips 2″ wide and piece together with diagonal seams to make a continuous binding strip. Press the seams open.

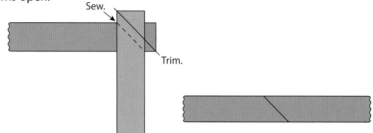

Press the entire strip in half lengthwise with wrong sides together. With raw edges even, pin the binding to the front edge of the quilt a few inches away from the corner, and leave the first few inches of the binding unattached. Start sewing, using a ¼″ seam allowance.

Stop ¼″ away from the first corner (see Step 1, below), and backstitch one stitch. Lift the presser foot and needle. Rotate the quilt one-quarter turn. Fold the binding at a right angle so it extends straight above the quilt and the fold forms a 45° angle in the corner (see Step 2). Then bring the binding strip down even with the edge of the quilt (see Step 3). Begin sewing at the folded edge. Repeat in the same manner at all corners.

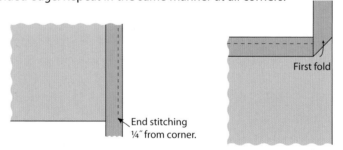

Step 1. Stitch to ¼″ from corner.

Step 2. First fold for miter

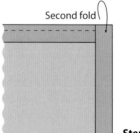

Step 3. Second fold alignment.

Continue stitching until you are back near the beginning of the binding strip. See Finishing the Binding Ends (page 107) for tips on finishing and hiding the raw edges of the ends of the binding.

Continuous Bias Binding

A continuous bias involves using a square sliced in half diagonally and then sewing the triangles together so that you continuously cut marked strips to make continuous bias binding. The same instructions can be used to cut bias for piping. Cut the fabric for the bias binding or piping so it is a square. For example, if yardage is ½ yard, cut an 18″ square. Cut the square in half diagonally, creating two triangles.

Sew these triangles together as shown, using a ¼″ seam allowance. Press the seam open.

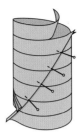

Straight grain

Bias   Bias

Using a ruler, mark the parallelogram with lines spaced the width you need to cut your bias. Cut along the first line about 5″.

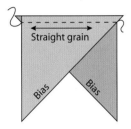

B   Side 1

Cut 5″.

A   Side 2

Join Side 1 and Side 2 to form a tube. Line A will line up with the raw edge at B. This will allow the first line to be offset by one strip width. Pin the raw ends together, making

sure that the lines match. Sew with a ¼″ seam allowance. Press the seam open. Cut along the drawn lines, creating one continuous strip.

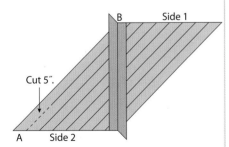

Press the entire strip in half lengthwise with wrong sides together. Place the binding on the quilt as described in Double-Fold Straight-Grain Binding (French Fold) (page 106).

See Finishing the Binding Ends for tips on finishing and hiding the raw edges of the ends of the binding.

Finishing the Binding Ends

Method 1:

After stitching around the quilt, fold under the beginning tail of the binding strip ¼″ so that the raw edge will be inside the binding after it is turned to the backside of the quilt. Place the end tail of the binding strip over the beginning folded end. Continue to attach the binding and stitch slightly beyond the starting stitches. Trim the excess binding. Fold the binding over the raw edges to the quilt back and hand stitch, mitering the corners.

Method 2:

Fold the ending tail of the binding back on itself where it meets the beginning binding tail. From the fold, measure and mark the cut width of your binding strip. Cut the ending binding tail to this measurement. For example, if your binding is cut 2¼″ wide, measure from the fold on the ending tail of the binding 2¼″ and cut the binding tail to this length.

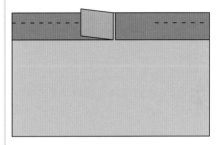

Fold, then cut binding tail to cut width of binding.

Open both tails. Place one tail on top of the other tail at right angles, right sides together. Mark a diagonal line and stitch on the line. Trim the seam to ¼″. Press open.

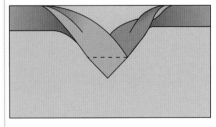

Stitch ends of binding diagonally.

Refold the binding and stitch this binding section in place on the quilt. Fold the binding over the raw edges to the quilt back and hand stitch, mitering the corners.

Flying Geese

The Flying Geese unit looks like two half-square triangles joined at the center, except there is no seam. Some sample finished sizes are 6″ × 3″ and 4″ × 2″. The unit can be made in several ways. The method given here involves some fabric waste but makes it easy for beginners to sew accurate diagonal seams. For each unit, you'll start with one rectangle and two squares.

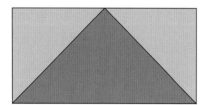

Block Diagram

1. Fold one B square diagonally in half and press lightly.

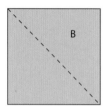 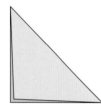

2. Unfold the square. Align it on one end of rectangle A, right sides together. Stitch on the diagonal fold line through both layers.

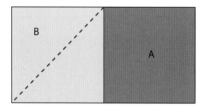

3. Trim off the excess ¼″ beyond the stitching line.

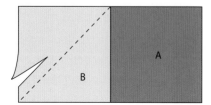

4. Fold the remaining triangular piece over the seam allowance and press from the right side.

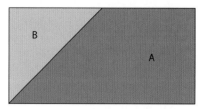

5. Repeat Steps 1–3 for the other side of rectangle A.

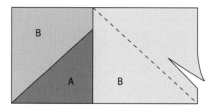

6. Fold back and press the second triangle. The overlapping seams at the top of the unit will disappear into the seam allowance when the unit is joined to other pieces.

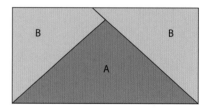

Paper Piecing

Once you get used to it, paper piecing is an easy way to ensure that your blocks will be accurate. You sew on the side of the paper with the printed lines. Fabric is placed on the nonprinted side.

1. Trace or photocopy the number of paper-piecing patterns needed for your project.

2. Use a smaller-than-usual stitch length (1.5–1.8 or 18 to 20 stitches per inch) and a slightly larger needle (size 90/14). This makes the paper removal easier, and will result in tighter stitches that can't be pulled apart when you tear off the paper.

3. Cut the pieces slightly larger than necessary—about ¾″ larger; they do not need to be perfect shapes. (One of the joys of paper piecing!)

With paper piecing you don't have to worry about the grain of the fabric. You are stitching on paper and that stabilizes the block. The paper is not torn off until after the blocks are stitched together.

4. Follow the number sequence when piecing. Pin piece #1 in place on the blank side of the paper, but make sure you don't place the pin anywhere near a seamline. Hold the paper up to the light to make sure the piece covers the area it is supposed to, with the seam allowance also amply covered.

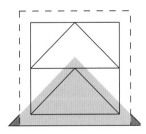

5. Fold the pattern back at the stitching line and trim the fabric to a ¼" seam allowance with a ruler and rotary cutter.

6. Cut piece #2 large enough to cover the area of #2 plus a generous seam allowance. It's a good idea to cut each piece larger than you think necessary; it might be a bit wasteful, but easier than ripping out tiny stitches! Align the edge with the trimmed seam allowance of piece #1, right sides together, and pin. Paper side up, stitch one line.

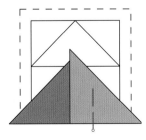

7. Open piece #2 and press.

8. Continue stitching each piece in order, being sure to fold back the paper pattern and trim the seam allowance to ¼" before adding the next piece.

9. Trim all around the finished unit to the ¼" seam allowance. Leave the paper intact until after the blocks have been sewn together, then carefully remove it. Creasing the paper at the seamline helps when tearing it.

paper-piecing hints

When making several identical blocks, it helps to work in assembly line fashion. Add pieces #1 and #2 to each of the blocks, then add #3, and so on.

Precutting all the pieces at once is a time saver. Make one block first to ensure that each fabric piece will cover the area needed.

When piecing a dark and a light fabric together, where the seam allowance needs to be pressed toward the light fabric, the edge of the dark seam allowance will sometimes show through the light fabric. To prevent this, trim the dark seam allowance about ¹⁄₁₆" narrower than the light seam allowance.

For additional help, go to:
www.ctpub.com > Consumer Resources > Quiltmaking Basics: Tips & Techniques for Quiltmaking & More

CONTRIBUTORS

Alex Anderson
Scrappy Triangles from *Finish It with Alex Anderson*

Alex's love affair with quiltmaking began in 1978, when she completed a Grandmother's Flower Garden quilt as part of her work toward a degree in art at San Francisco State University. Over the years, her focus has rested on understanding fabric relationships and on an intense appreciation for traditional quilting surface design and star quilts.

For eleven years, Alex hosted television's premier quilt show *Simply Quilts* and is currently co-host, along with Ricky Tims, of the Internet-based The Quilt Show. She is also a spokesperson for Bernina of America. Her quilts have appeared in numerous magazines, often in articles devoted specifically to her work.

Visit Alex's website at www.alexandersonquilts.com.

Peggy J. Barkle
Curvaceous Cabin from *Blendable Curves*

Peggy was born in Seattle, Washington, but grew up in the San Francisco Bay Area. She attended high school in San Francisco and studied interior design in college. When she came across a PBS series on quilting hosted by Eleanor Burns, she had run through every craft known to man (or woman). But when she put fabric between her fingers, the search was over. She was hooked, she was home!

She began teaching in 1995 at a local quilt shop and area guilds. Her favorite students are the beginners, wide-eyed and eager. She has a room full of yardage and a brain full of ideas. She could not imagine doing anything else and considers being able to share what she loves an unbelievable blessing.

Visit Peggy's website at www.peggybarkle.com.

Karen Dugas
Sunshine and Windmills from *Mary Mashuta's Confetti Quilts*

Karen is a dedicated quilter whose work has appeared in local quilt shows and several of Mary Mashuta's books. She teaches quilting classes at her local quilt shop.

Becky Goldsmith
Goose in the Pond from *Piecing the Piece O' Cake Way*
Birds of a Feather from *Amish-Inspired Quilts*

Becky is one half of Piece O' Cake Designs (along with Linda Jenkins, co-author of the above books). While most known for their wonderful appliqué, Becky also loves to piece.

Becky's degree in interior design and her many art classes provided a perfect background for quilting. Becky and Linda have shown many quilts and have won numerous awards. Together they make a dynamic quilting duo and love to teach other quilters the joys of appliqué and piecing.

Visit Becky's website at www.pieceocake.com.

Margrit Hall
Coming Storms from *Bennie Harper's Quilt Album*

Margrit began teaching quilting in 1982, first at Heritage Quilt Store in Cheyenne, Wyoming, then at Laramie County Community College in Cheyenne. She specializes in quilting history and design technique.

She designs original quilts and patterns under the name Cat Tail Designs. Her creations combine her love of watercolor painting with the feel and freedom of expression provided by fabric. Her original patterns have been published in many quilting publications, and she continues to be one of the featured quilt designers in the new *Better Homes and Gardens* quilt catalog. Her quilts have also been shown in invitational gallery exhibits.

Visit Margrit's website at www.cattaildesigns.com.

Dixie Haywood
Pleiades Pineapples from *Shoreline Quilts*,
edited by Cyndy Lyle Rymer

Dixie has taught quiltmaking since 1974. She has authored, co-authored, and contributed to many books. Her articles and designs appear regularly in national quilting magazines.

Diana McClun and Laura Nownes
Winter Flowers from *Q Is for Quilts*

Diana and Laura are authors of a number of quilting books, including *Quilts! Quilts!! Quilts!!!* and *Quilts, Quilts, and More Quilts!*

The pair has worked together on television programs, with study groups, and in seminars touching thousands of students, giving them a start in the basics of quiltmaking. They founded Teacher Development Seminars as a result of their commitment to the continuing education of quiltmaking, and currently create patterns under the name From You to Me.

Visit Diana and Laura at their website, www.dianaandlaura.com.

Lerlene Nevaril
Autumn Richness from *Hidden Block Quilts*

After developing an interest in quilting, Lerlene organized a quilt guild in Sioux City, Iowa, and served as its first president. She began teaching in 1985 and then in 1996 opened a quilt shop, Heart and Hand Dry Goods. She has appeared on *Simply Quilts* and has taught and lectured throughout the central United States.

Visit Lerlene's website at www.lerlenenevaril.com.

Nancy Odom
Vinnie's Double Pinwheel from *Elm Creek Quilts*

Quilt designer, author, and teacher Nancy Odom teamed up with Jennifer Chiaverini on *Elm Creek Quilts*. She has 27 patterns and 6 books in publication, with more pattern and book ideas always in the works. Also among her creations are Quilter's Gloves for the machine quilter. Her company, Timid Thimble Creations, markets her products.

Nancy has appeared on *Simply Quilts* with Alex Anderson and on *America Sews with Sue Hausmann*. Her quilts have appeared in national quilting magazines, and she is a featured teacher and lecturer at quilt shows, quilt guilds, and quilt shops around the country.

Visit Nancy's website at www.timidthimble.com.

Claudia Olson
Castle Weather from *15 Two-Block Quilts*

Never content to leave a quilt in is simplest form, Claudia has always looked for ways to make it more interesting. Her fascination with two-block quilts was sparked when she was a student of Marsha McClosky. After developing some of her own methods and ideas, she began sharing them through teaching quilt classes and presentations to her local quilt group.

Gai Perry
Making Waves and *A-Tisket, A-Tasket, I've Got an Extra Basket!* from *24 Quilted Gems*

Gai began her romance with quilting in 1981. In 1985 she started teaching color and design at local quilt shops and seminars. Because of her fondness for antiques, her focus was on making traditional-style quilts. By 1990 she had a desire to start painting again, but instead of working with brushes, she developed an original style of quilting she named "The Art of the Impressionist Landscape." With the publication of *24 Quilted Gems,* Gai says she is absolutely, positively going to get back into painting. We know all her students hope that she will take time out to teach classes and write more books!

Donna Ingram Slusser
Jewel Box from *Shadow Quilts*

Patricia Maixner Magaret and Donna Ingram Slusser enjoy an active quilting partnership that has developed over a period of twenty years. They are co-authors of several best-selling books, including *Shadow Quilts.*

Jan Bode Smiley
Courthouse Blues from *Focus on Batiks*

Jan Bode Smiley is the author of four books and continues to enjoy the process and discovery of creating work for publication. Jan is currently working with many different media, including fabric, paint, wood, paper, and found objects.

She began her artistic life as a quiltmaker and continues to build on those skills while experimenting with other art forms. She loves to share her interest in merging media and teaches workshops internationally.

Visit Jan's website at www.jansmiley.com.

Pam Stallebrass
Tropical Butterflies from *Simple Stenciling*

Pam's two passions are crafts and travel. She lives near Cape Town, South Africa. In her home studio, she dyes and prints fabric, which she sells regularly at quilt shows. She writes articles on quiltmaking for *Patchwork* and *Quilting, UK.*

Laura Wasilowski
Lazy Log Cabin from *Fusing Fun*

Laura Wasilowski loves fabric. Her first love was a sweet pink gingham fabric selected for a 4-H sewing project. As a college student, she discovered more exotic fabrics. And while she earned a degree in costume design, she found a new thrill—dyeing.

For many years Laura created hand-dyed fabrics for garments that she sold in boutiques across the country. It was a friendly neighbor who introduced Laura to her current flame, the art quilt. This latest love is a marriage of fabric, color, and whimsy that she truly enjoys.

Visit Laura's website at www.artfabrik. com.

Rebecca Wat
Bow Tie Medley from *A Fresh Twist on Fabric Folding*

Rebecca Wat is an origami expert and quilt designer. Her idea to apply origami techniques to quilting has resulted in the birth of a new kind of three-dimensional quilt. She has appeared on HGTV to demonstrate her techniques. Her work has been featured by various domestic and foreign quilting magazines, as well as in international quilt shows and museums. Rebecca also knits and has written a book of easy-to-knit projects.

Jean Wells
Summer Fun and *Favorite Quilt* from *Patchwork Quilts Made Easy*

This prolific author of 28 books, teacher, and shop owner is well known in the quilting world for her willingness to share ideas for quilting as well as teaching business workshops. She established one of the first quilt shops in the United States, The Stitchin' Post, in 1975 in Sisters, Oregon. The same year she started the world-famous Sisters Outdoor Quilt Show.

She has won numerous awards: Business of the Year in Sisters, Citizen of the Year, the Michael Kile Award for Lifetime Achievement, and the Imagination Award for *Paradise in the Garden* in the 2000 Millenium Quilt Contest, and was the first independent retailer to be inducted into the Primedia Hall of Fame.

Visit Jean's store at www.stitchinpost.com.

Joen Wolfrom
A Splash of Tulips from *A Garden Party of Quilts*

Joen began quiltmaking in 1974. She has taught and lectured in the quilting field, both nationally and internationally, since 1984. In the 1980s, Joen created commissioned textile art for many private clients and corporations. Her work is included in collections throughout the world. Joen is the author of nine books and products. Several have been bestsellers in the arts and crafts field.

Joen is the owner of JWD Publishing, a pattern company that publishes designs by leading quiltmakers and designers. These patterns may be purchased at quilt and fabric stores under each designer's pattern-line name.

Visit Joen's website at www.jwdpublishing.com.

Great Titles *from* C&T PUBLISHING

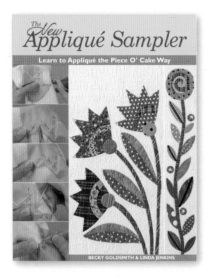

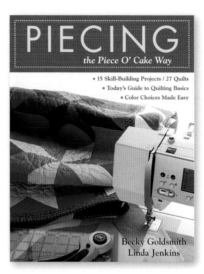

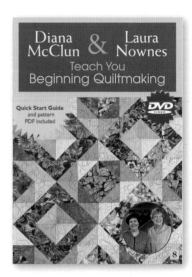

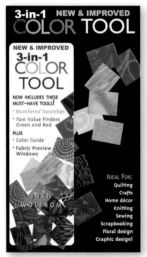

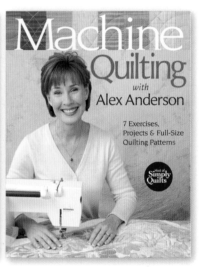

Available at your local retailer or **www.ctpub.com** *or* **800.284.1114**

For a list of other fine books from C&T Publishing, ask for a free catalog:

C&T PUBLISHING, INC.
P.O. Box 1456
Lafayette, CA 94549
(800) 284-1114

Email: ctinfo@ctpub.com
Website: www.ctpub.com

C&T Publishing's professional photography services are now available to the public. Visit us at www.ctmediaservices.com.

Tips and Techniques can be found at www.ctpub.com > Consumer Resources > Quiltmaking Basics: Tips & Techniques for Quiltmaking & More

For quilting supplies:

COTTON PATCH
1025 Brown Ave.
Lafayette, CA 94549
Store: (925) 284-1177
Mail order: (925) 283-7883

Email: CottonPa@aol.com
Website: www.quiltusa.com

Note: Fabrics used in the quilts shown may not be currently available, as fabric manufacturers keep most fabrics in print for only a short time.